# How

## to Be a

## Hepburn

## in a

## Kardashian

## World

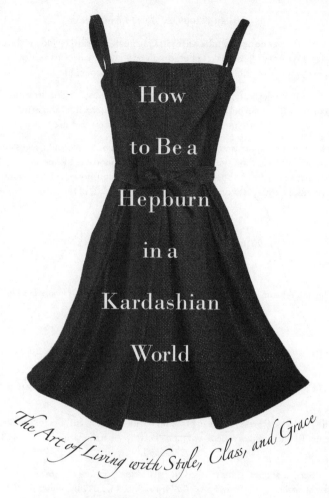

How

to Be a

Hepburn

in a

Kardashian

World

*The Art of Living with Style, Class, and Grace*

# Jordan Christy

**CENTER STREET**

New York  Boston  Nashville

Center Street
Hachette Book Group
1290 Avenue of the Americas, New York, NY 1010
centerstreet.com
twitter.com/centerstreet

The first edition of this book was published as *How to Be a Hepburn in a Hilton World*.

Revised Edition: April 2017

Center Street is a division of Hachette Book Group, Inc. The Center Street name and logo are trademarks of Hachette Book Group, Inc.

The publisher is not responsible for websites (or their content) that are not owned by the publisher.

The Hachette Speakers Bureau provides a wide range of authors for speaking events. To find out more, go to www.HachetteSpeakersBureau.com or call (866) 376-6591.

Scripture quotations marked NIV are taken from *The Holy Bible, New International Version*®. Copyright © 1973, 1978, 1984, 2011 by Biblica, Inc.® Used by permission. All rights reserved worldwide.

Scripture quotations marked MSG are taken from *The Message*. Copyright © 1993, 1994, 1995, 1996, 2000, 2001, 2002. Used by permission of NavPress Publishing Group.

LCCN: 2017932177

ISBNs: 978-1-4555-9866-3 (hardcover); 978-1-4555-9867-0 (ebook)

Printed in the United States of America

LSC-C

10 9 8 7 6 5 4 3 2 1

# Contents

# Introduction

"Sometimes you need a second chance, because you weren't quite ready for the first."—*Anonymous*

Seven years ago, I wrote a book called *How to Be a Hepburn in a Hilton World*, a project I was confident would sell exactly four copies (to my family—I figured they'd each buy a copy out of sheer obligation), and that would be the end of such a random endeavor. You see, I'd played music my whole life, moved to Nashville when I was nineteen to pursue a career in the music industry, and was lucky enough to get a job at an amazing record label my senior year of college. My husband and I also got married that year and bought our first house. Life was good.

So it was to my surprise and complete shock when I suddenly became a "writer." Beyond penning our family's annual Christmas letter and a pithy entry in my college's literary journal, I'd never had the slightest tendency toward a career in books. Not only was it new and exciting, but it seemed to be a nice little addition to my great day job. I signed my first contract when I was twenty-three years old, and I was completely self-assured. When I sat down to work on the book that summer, I knew exactly what I wanted to write about.

To properly tell the rest of the story, we need to back up about a decade. When I was thirteen, I started attending a new middle school along with several of my friends from elementary. I was actually really excited about the new school and making new friends, as it was a much bigger class than I'd grown up with. However, a few kids, for whatever reason, took it upon themselves to make sure that never happened and set out to make my life miserable. I would come to school in the morning and open my locker, only to find it filled with trash. I remember standing there, day after day, trying not to cry, as I picked up all the garbage that had spilled out into the hallway. I told myself, *Whatever you do, don't cry. Or you'll forever be* that *kid who cried in seventh grade.* At the end of the day, they would scream hateful things outright and throw cans and bottles at me during the bus ride home. Every day just got worse, and by the end of the year, I begged my mom to pull me out of school and just homeschool me.

It was a lonely time, and I remember wishing that I just had someone, anyone, to talk to. I now know, as an adult, that people can just be mean for no reason whatsoever (myself included, as I would soon come to find), but as a thirteen-year-old, it felt like I was the only target of hate in the world. I occasionally caught glimpses of what was being said about me, and it would only make the tears come quicker. So I trained myself to simply survive; if I could make it through the day without crying, I considered the day a success. By the time I got to high school, I vowed that if I ever had the opportunity, I would write a book for that girl I'd been—the one walking the halls by herself every day, the one with no one to sit by at lunch, the one fighting back tears during seventh-period biology. I would write something to make her feel like she had at least *one* friend in the world, even if it was just a book.

I would write a book that would give that girl the confidence to keep her chin up; a book that would give her the strength to get through the next day; a book that just might make her laugh and smile, even if nothing else in life was happy or good. I resolved to forever be an advocate for any girl who'd ever been the *only one*—the *only one* without a partner on frog dissection day, the *only one* who wasn't invited to Amy W.'s birthday party, the *only one* who didn't get picked for the kickball team. I wanted that girl to know she wasn't alone—I wanted her to know that someone out there had been through the same thing, but that someone had gone on to have an amazing life. I wanted her to know that who you are in middle school (or high school or college) doesn't have to define who you are for the rest of your life.

So, when I sat down to write my first book that summer I turned twenty-three, I knew exactly what I wanted to say. Except it didn't come out exactly as I'd planned. You see, other than my mom, I'd never told anyone what happened to me in junior high. Not a soul. I stuffed those tears and hurt and rejection down so far that I'd never have to deal with them ever again. It hurt enough the first time going through it—why would I want to talk about it ever again?

Little did I know, those things have a way of coming out in one form or another, at some point. The unfortunate thing was that all those suppressed, toxic emotions spilled out into one tiny book. All the hurt, all the anger, and all the pain came out in a neat, succinct little package that was then shipped to every major bookstore and translated into several different languages. By the time I realized what had unconsciously spilled out, it was too late.

Suddenly, I was the mean one. I had said things that I regretted and hurt people that I'd never meant to hurt. Even innocent celebrities somehow got swept up in the wake of my unspoken pain. The strange thing is, I'm actually an unbelievably (okay, obnoxiously) bubbly, optimistic, and kind person—I love people and always go out of my way to make sure everyone feels loved and valued and included. But by reading that book, you'd assume I was nothing but angry and bitter. Turns out, there's a small part of me that still was.

It's no secret that the world has changed drastically in the few years since that first book was published (Snapchat happened; *The Hunger Games* happened; Miley Cyrus happened), but the biggest change for me took place in my heart. I begged God for a chance to go back and make things right. I had never meant to hurt anyone. I knew I had to find the girls I'd written about and ask for forgiveness. I was able to track down one girl in particular, who had actually been my friend prior to the whole junior high ordeal. I e-mailed her and asked if she could find it in her heart to forgive me for all the ickiness that had taken place. To my surprise, she e-mailed back and said that she, too, had wanted to send a similar e-mail—she had thought many times about looking me up to say sorry. She extended forgiveness (which I was more than happy to accept), and within a few short e-mail exchanges and pictures of our current lives and families, all was forgotten. The horribleness from the past was gone and our friendship was restored. I broke down crying in a flood of relief. I ended by telling her that if I ever had the chance to rewrite the book, I would.

As luck would have it, two months later, my agent called and said my publisher was interested in publishing a second edition of the book. I knew it was the second chance I'd been praying for. The Kardashians had come to fame and were an obvious topic for debate, as they are inarguably the A-list representatives of our generation. However, my heart had changed and I knew I could never speak another critical word about anyone—even if it was a far-off celebrity I would probably never meet. Suddenly, I felt overwhelming compassion for anyone who'd ever been scrutinized by the media, or who'd been defined by one or two comments they made offhand. No matter who they were, or what they stood for, I just couldn't make them the bad guys.

I discovered that the celebrities we put on a pedestal and then so flippantly criticize seem a whole lot closer after you've been called out for your own flaws and insecurities on a national scale. Feeling scorn and judgment from the world at large is a heavy weight to carry and I wouldn't wish it on anyone. Which brings me back to the Kardashians. Love them or hate them, they have collectively, and individually, absorbed their share of scrutiny. Being the constant target of criticism and opinion is an enormous thing to work through, and for that, I admire them. Though their style may be different from mine, or Audrey Hepburn's (or whatever celebrity name you want to throw out there), they're still human beings and deserve my respect. So, with that, this is not an "Us vs. Them" book—it's not an argument for, or against, any one person. It's not a guidebook on how to be perfect. It's simply my attempt to go back and write the book I always wanted to—a book for any girl who's ever felt like *the only one*.

What do you do when you find yourself *the only one*? The only one who didn't make the team, the only one who didn't get called for an interview, the only one without a date to prom? I've now lived long enough to know that it's not just in junior high you can feel like *the only one*; it can be at your sorority house, at your first job, at your twenty-fifth birthday party…It can happen when you least expect it, from the people you least expect it from. Which, I think, makes it all the more difficult to recover from. In my case, it took only sixteen short years to get over! (I really should have titled this book *Learn from My Mistakes So You Don't Waste Half Your Life*.)

The other bad thing about not getting over a grievance is

that, in some form or another, the original offense continues to perpetuate itself. Have you ever heard the phrase "Hurt people hurt people"? Well, later in life, I found myself doing the very thing I hated—I deliberately excluded girls and said hurtful things, for no apparent reason whatsoever. You see, in whatever way you were hurt, that behavior just might continue to pop up in your life until it's dealt with. See? I *told* you I should have titled it *Learn from My Mistakes So You Don't Waste Half Your Life*.

If you've currently, or at any point in your life, found yourself to be *the only one*, I have a few survival tips—fresh from the school of hard knocks. May this list bring you good fortune and see you working through your issues in under a decade!

* **Stay in the light**—There is a universal characteristic and goal of pain and it is this: to keep you in the dark. Being hurt makes you feel like you can't, and don't want to, talk to anyone. It forces you to wallow through each day in silent misery, telling you that no one understands and it will never get better. Well, I'm here to tell you, that's a lie. The truth is, you're still you, regardless of your circumstances. You can go back there tomorrow and be your vibrant, joyful self. No matter what anybody says and no matter what anybody thinks, be *you*. You don't have to hide in the shadows; stay in the light.

* **Find a way to laugh**—I recently went through a really intense health crisis and my mom's advice was this: Find a

way to laugh at least once a day. That was my prescription. Things can feel really dark when you're walking through a hard time, and sometimes you just have to lighten your own load. Download your favorite childhood movie, find a comedian on YouTube, or just call up a funny friend. Force yourself to smile and enjoy part of the day, every day.

* **Go to your happy place**—When the majority of your day is pervaded by your problem (i.e., the issue at work, school, home, or some other place you're forced to be several hours out of the day), it's essential to find an outside outlet. Our church's youth group was always my happy place, because I knew it was a safe zone—no one from my class attended there, and I was able to develop an amazing group of outside friends completely separate from school. No matter how bleak the rest of the week was, I always knew Thursday nights would be good. Find an activity that requires escape—maybe it's a pottery class, a book club, or a volunteer job at a women's shelter. Just find some way to get away from your routine and your current situation.

* **Make the most of it**—If you're going to be hanging out by yourself for a while, you might as well make the most of it. I just so happened to be involved in piano, so I proceeded to pour myself into it, day and night—and lo and behold, I got pretty good at it. Not that I have anything to show for it these days, but the fact remains that I got a lot of joy and fulfillment out of those hours (okay, years) of extra practice. It doesn't have to be a musical instrument, though—just use

that time to better yourself or the world around you. You could organize a lecture series at your local library, offer to teach Sunday school, or learn how to cook. You never know what lifelong skill you might develop!

* **Don't let yourself become bitter**—The strange thing about my situation was that by the time I got to high school, things had improved greatly. I made a lot of really great friends, was involved in countless activities, and was even voted class president. But deep down, I was really just counting the days until I could leave for college and never see that initial group of mean kids ever again. Though the bullying had stopped, I (clearly) had never gotten over it. Again, don't waste half your life being bitter about something that's in the past.

* **Step out of your comfort zone**—Let's be honest, it's hard to step out and make new friends when all you want to do is curl up in the corner with a pint of Rocky Road. It takes a lot of work to develop new friendships when everything is going *right*, so it takes even more effort to get out of your comfort zone and forge new relationships when you're feeling hurt and insecure, but forge you must. It's the only way to move forward. I'm still so thankful for the sweet friendships that were formed during that time.

* *Forgiveness* **can become a four-letter word**—I can't tell you how many times I uttered the phrase "I forgive so-and-so..." begrudgingly under my breath. I knew forgiving those kids was the right thing to do, but in actuality, it played out

like this: "Well, I've forgiven them...but I still kind of hate them." At the risk of sounding ooey-gooey, world-peacey, I discovered that real forgiveness takes you from a place of begrudging to empathy. Because once you realize that the person who hurt you probably went through something much worse than you did to make them act that way, it makes you feel compassion for them...even sympathy. It makes it easy to forgive because it's the simple realization that we're all human and we've all messed up. So don't withhold forgiveness from somebody—it doesn't hold the other person hostage, it keeps *you* down. Turn your bad situation into a *good* four-letter word, like *love*.

Most of us have encountered setbacks and obstacles in life. But it's not the problem itself that determines the rest of our lives—it's our *reaction* to the problem. Because everyone's hurdles look different—some might have health complications, others may be dealing with friend issues, and still others might be going through a family split or battling depression. Whatever the obstacle is, it's just that—an obstacle. Something to be climbed over, run around, or conquered. It's not the end of your story or the final outcome of your life—it's simply a challenge. And when you rise to the challenge and meet it head-on to the best of your ability, you'll be amazed at the strength you'll find within yourself. You'll also be shocked at how much wisdom and perspective you'll have after you've come through it on the other side. Your attitude and reaction will determine the outcome.

When you go through a hard time, it's easy to identify yourself with the source of your pain. Sometimes it can be hard to see your life past your current situation so you make self-identifying statements like: "I have an autoimmune disease," "I don't have any friends," or "I'm suicidal." But *you* are not your *problem*. There's more to you than cancer, or new stepsiblings, or that car accident. You've got a whole life and personality outside of your difficulty, so be careful not to eternally brand yourself as "sick," "a loser," or "stupid." These temporary issues are fleeting, and you'll have the rest of your beautiful life to live on the other side of your challenge. Don't permanently label yourself with something that was meant to be only a temporary blip on the radar of your life.

And finally, see yourself as an overcomer. I didn't know, as a seventh grader fighting back tears and praying to get through the day, that I'd one day be writing books and speaking to thousands of young women. I never saw that coming in a million years. But I did see myself as one thing: an overcomer. I knew I was smart and fun, and I could see myself eventually making new friends. I could see myself having a successful career as a musician or songwriter (granted, that went by the wayside, but it gave me a lot of inspiration and motivation at the time). I could see myself having a husband, a career, and a family. I knew, deep down, that there was more to me than

Introduction

horrible bus rides and hiding out in the bathroom. But I had to see it, and the same will be true for you. You have to visualize yourself beyond your current circumstances—see yourself as already having beat this thing!

Several years ago, the beautiful and talented Lauren Scruggs Kennedy endured a traumatic accident—after stepping into the propeller of an airplane, she lost her left eye and left hand. Though she had a successful career as a model and worked in the fashion industry prior to her accident, she feared that her life was over because of her changed appearance. In reality, she says, "I gained a new perspective on life... I just want to use what I've been through to talk to young girls and let them know our appearance is not what defines us."[1] Lauren is now married to the adorable Jason Kennedy and runs a successful blog that covers fashion, food, and fitness. She is an amazing example of not letting your tragedy define who you are.

So when you think you're the *only one*, just remember— you're *never* the only one. There's a whole sisterhood of women out there who might be going through the same thing you are or something similar. You *will* get through this, and you'll be a better person because of it. Just smile, hold your head high, and be you.

# How

# to Be a

# Hepburn

# in a

# Kardashian

# World

*Chapter One*

# The Illusion of Perfection

"Charm is deceptive, and beauty is fleeting."
—*Proverbs 31:30* (NIV)

I need to make a confession: I'm not graceful, demure, or delicate. In fact, I'm messy, disorganized, and kind of loud. I trip and fall more than any other person I know, and I usually spend the majority of my days in sweatpants. Not exactly the stuff etiquette books are made of. But the really unfortunate thing is that the more I *try* to be an ideal person— classy, intelligent, stylish, successful—the more my efforts fall laughably short. Perfection, it would seem, is an illusion.

The phrase "nobody's perfect" sounds good in theory, yet we tend to reserve it strictly for ourselves when we've made a colossal mistake or irreversibly screwed something up. It rarely applies to anyone else—and certainly not to the people whose faces we see on magazines. *Her* body is flawless. *Their* lives are perfect. We are apt to put media figures on a pedestal and elevate them to near-godlike status. But even the most accomplished and graceful people in the world are still just human. Perfection is still just an illusion.

Consider Audrey Hepburn. Princess Diana. Mother Teresa. These were inarguably some of the most beloved women of the twentieth century. They were not perfect, but they were beloved. True, each of them was accomplished, intelligent, and classy, but ultimately, it wasn't their outward appearance that caused them to be honored and respected by millions. It was their heart. Their talent. Their generosity. Their love for people. These are the attributes we remember about someone long after their haircut has gone out of style or smile lines have taken over their face. That's what we remember after the illusion of perfection has worn off.

And yet we still try to assign perfection to people. We place them on an unattainable echelon and proceed to sniff at our own shortcomings by comparison. We point out our inadequacies while elevating their laudable attributes. We love to have a standard by which we can measure perfection, even if it's not us.

We annually determine the planet's most beautiful men and women in the tabloids with a somewhat fame-based yardstick. Boys have their own numerical ranking system for girls: "She's a 10!"; "She's a 4." And then there are, of course, the little judgments we make about ourselves and one another all day long: "Her hair is perfect!"; "I look terrible today."

Most of these classifications are based on temporal observations and conditions. They are all subject to change. Nothing about us—our flaws or even our favorite aspects—is going to last. So if perfection is an illusion, and this outer shell of ours is deteriorating even as we speak, then it would have to mean that life is more about what's on the inside—our intellect, our character, our heart—than our false lashes and spray tans (don't get me wrong, I love a good spray tan). But if that's true (and I think we would all agree with the old adage "It's what on the inside that counts"), how does that actually play out on a day-to-day basis? What does that look like when you're constantly bombarded with bikini triangles, explicit song lyrics, and the glamorous lives of celebs like the Kardashians? It seems like a huge chasm to bridge—we're expected to cultivate a thoughtful, intelligent, beautiful inner life and yet fit in with the loud, wild, uncensored world around us? How does that work? What does it look like?

I think it starts by reworking our definition of *beauty*. Because if we constantly judge ourselves according to the world's standards and "their" definition of beauty, we will never measure up (who are "they" anyway?). We will continuously be trying to fill that material vacuum in our lives. In that light, I propose a change to our mental dictionaries: Instead of defining *beauty* as the hottest reality star with the best hair extensions, perhaps we could tweak that definition to include one's wisdom, attitude, and character. I've met some people who are drop-dead gorgeous, but their attitude stinks (you know someone like that too, don't you?). And sure enough, little by little, that person becomes not-so-pretty in your eyes. On the other hand, I've had a couple of colleagues and acquaintances with off-the-charts humor, intelligence, and work ethics. I would describe them to anyone as beautiful people, just because I know their hearts.

The definition of beauty, therefore, seems to be quite malleable. If it can change within hours or days based on our own experience with someone, just think how it can shift on a global scale. It usually plays out something like this...pop star/TV sensation/business mogul/(insert your own celebrity example here) has a rocketlike ascent to fame and is quickly beloved and accepted by everyone. They are hailed as the best new thing: the world's most beautiful person. At the first sign of trouble, however—an ill-timed single, an unfortunate PR story, a style blunder—the media, fans, and world turn on them and declare them a has-been. They're no longer relevant and, therefore, no longer beautiful. It's sad but true, and I'm sorry to say that I've been part of the problem—throwing stones on one side and lying facedown in the gutter on the other. We all have been affected, or been the cause, to some degree—whether it's junior high politics, mean girl behavior, or just finger-pointing at our own TVs—we're all quite fickle with one another.

What if we committed to defining beauty over the course of time—say, something longer than a pep rally or a run of fifteen minutes of fame? Because it seems to me that things with the strongest foundation also have the most staying power. People and things that are "here today, gone tomorrow" are a dime a dozen. But when you think back on the women who have made the greatest impact over the past century, who comes to mind? Eleanor Roosevelt. Oprah Winfrey. Marie Curie. These women and their accomplishments have endured for *decades*. Through style changes, political climates, and cultural differences, their messages have proved strong enough to endure. They've contributed something. They've left the world a better place. How does one stand the test of time? What qualities are necessary to leave a legacy?

I've been thinking about the classics a lot lately. I love classic books and have fallen in love with them all over again while reading them with my kids (they will be experts on *The Chronicles of Narnia* by the time they leave for college if I have anything to say about it!). But what makes a book a classic? What makes a handful of literary works endure for decades and centuries? Why do some live on while countless others fall by the wayside?

There is a certain standard by which we can test things—the test of time. I daresay we could throw our new definition of *beauty* in with the same criteria. Why? It seems to me that thousands of aesthetically pleasing women have come and gone throughout history, but only a few have been revered and remembered. Think about who has made a greater impact on you personally—an actor you were in love with for a summer during high school (here's looking at you, Philip Kiriakis), or your favorite author whose every new book you devour? The teacher you had for one semester, or your grandmother who always let you help her in the kitchen? The people who leave the greatest mark on our lives usually do so over the course of time.

Likewise, the women who have made history—Margaret Thatcher, Rosa Parks, Abigail Adams—didn't do so because of the eyeliner they used or the brand of running shoes they endorsed. They made an impact on humanity because they made a conscious choice and effort to stand up for what they believed in: Goodness. Justice. Love. These are the truths that change the world.

Do you know of any classic books that have endured solely based on their cover? Most of them don't even have the original art or graphics, if there were any to begin with. The content that gives the book enduring qualities is contained within the pages—the inside. I think people are the same way. It's not our cover art, so to speak, that the world remembers about us (dear Lord, I hope they don't remember mine...mine would consist of two-inch roots and sweatpants); it's our generosity, acts of kindness, and our hearts that create a legacy.

What do you love most about your best friend? Is it her waist size or her sense of humor? What about your sister? Is your favorite thing her thoughtfulness or her shoe collection? How about your favorite teacher? Was it the skirts she wore or the life lessons she taught you? The things we love about one another aren't typically the fleeting, outward things. They're almost always intangible things.

The other day, my four-year-old son asked, "Mama, do you

know what the difference is between pretty and beautiful?" Somewhat bewildered by such a deep, probing question, I stammered around that I, in fact, did not know. He then proceeded to patiently explain:

"Well, pretty means you're wearing something fancy, but beautiful means you love someone." He smiled proudly, then added, "And I love you, so you're beautiful."

I squeezed that boy so hard his eyeballs almost popped out. I told him that was the perfect definition: Beautiful *does* mean you love someone. Because when you love someone, they become beautiful to you, no matter what they actually look like. It was the sweetest, simplest way of saying, *Beauty is in the eye of the beholder.*

I'm sorry to say that it took a long time for me to finally learn this truth. A few years ago, I felt close to being on top of the world. I had nice clothes, a wonderful family, offers pouring in, and friends in high places. What else could you want? I couldn't see how all that material "stuff" was really just a house of cards waiting to fall. I had been sick for a while, and I was eventually diagnosed with several debilitating diseases over the course of the next two years. I spent much of that time on the couch or in bed, as I was unable to walk or even hold my kids most days, and I was secretly devastated about my appearance and the loss of my lifestyle.

But a funny thing happens when you're looking at life with the possibility of being deformed and disfigured—suddenly everything nonessential in your life becomes meaningless. It makes you want to kiss your kids' sticky little faces, call up your best friend and tell her why you love her, and send your mom some flowers just because she's your mom. My tears of pain and self-pity eventually turned into tears of joy when I looked around and saw that I had everything I needed—my sweet babies were toddling around me on the floor, all of our family lived near us, and my husband loved me. I realized God had not abandoned me; in fact, he was right there beside me.

It took being unable to walk or turn doorknobs to make me realize that no movie deals or designer dresses or book contracts could save me. I had previously put my hope in my career, my abilities, my material worth; but, in that moment, I finally realized that none of those things could really help me. It was a painful relief. A wonderful, ugly truth. A beautiful letdown, if you will.

I began to find so much beauty in simple, daily tasks that the beauty found on Instagram suddenly became a distant second. First-class tickets and five-star hotels were nothing compared to a Cheerio-filled car seat. Trying on designer shoes was not as sweet as hearing my husband play a song on his guitar. My legs barely worked, my stomach couldn't tolerate most foods, and I wasn't even able to wash my own hair—and yet, I felt like the luckiest girl in the world. As it turned out, perfection wasn't a prerequisite for happiness.

What's your definition of *perfection*? What's your definition of *beauty*? If it's anything more than you, just as you are, then it's probably an illusion. Because the way I see it, you can dress yourself up all you want, get new cheekbones, dye your hair, and make yourself aesthetically perfect, but most people don't care. *I* don't care. You don't have to be perfect to be happy, successful, or loved. My family still loved me when I missed birthdays and holidays that year, my husband still loved me when I could no longer go on dates, and God still loved me when I couldn't even shower (it doesn't get much uglier than that, folks). Think about those who love you—it might be family and friends, it might be someone who passed on or even a beloved pet. Just knowing that you're loved makes you feel innately beautiful. And when you know you're loved, you don't feel the need to go drumming up business, so to speak, somewhere else. You can simply rest in the fact that you're *you*—freckles, broad shoulders, stubby fingers, and all.

It's okay if you don't have a date this Friday because you know that you, all by yourself, are enough. It's all right if your little black dress from tenth grade doesn't fit quite right anymore because you know that the life lessons and experiences you've gained along the way count for more than those ten pounds. It's okay if you don't have Kim Kardashian's lashes or Carrie Underwood's legs or Emma Watson's haircut (although I'd like all three). *You* are the definition of *perfect*—imperfections and all.

## Chapter Two

# Social Media Etiquette

"Manners are a sensitive awareness of the feelings of
others. If you have that awareness, you have good manners, no matter what fork you use." —*Emily Post*[2]

Social media etiquette: It's almost an oxymoron, right?
Between all the tweets and pokes and likes and comments, it's hard to know which way is up and which
way's down. One day we're soaring with eagles over the
fifteen-plus likes and compliments on our new profile pic, and
the next day we're hunched over the keypad in a puddle of
our own tears. *My boyfriend's online, but he didn't comment on
my post...does he even like me? I sent a message to that girl saying I'm sorry...did she even get it? My hair salon pic only got two
likes...does it look bad???* It can be an emotional roller-coaster
ride when it comes to social media, and it would be naive to
think that all the world's problems could be solved with a few
how-to's. But, on the flip side, following polite online protocol
can potentially help you score your dream job, communicate
with long-lost friends, or discover a lifelong, meaningful rela-

tionship (*You've Got Mail*, anyone?). So don't throw the baby out with the bathwater just yet. Wait until I use a few more idioms first.

Have you noticed how, in person, people are usually mindful and show consideration for others' thoughts and feelings? We go above and beyond to make sure others feel loved and comfortable around us. But suddenly, when we get online, it can be like Thunderdome! Anything goes! I call this phenomenon *video-game syndrome*. Have you ever played, or watched someone play, one of those car chase games? You'd run your car off a cliff or crash it into a brick wall and that would be that. The loser music would sound (wohn-wohn-*wohhhn*) and the game would end. If you were to drive a car like that in real life, it would be disastrous, but for some reason we know it's okay to do it online because *it's not real*. I think we have the same perception with social media today—sometimes it's hard to imagine a real human on the other side of our screen, with a beating heart and thoughts and feelings. It all seems somewhat make-believe.

We're living in the age of safety helmets and seat belts, but when it comes to our words, we can be quite harsh and hurtful (I'm preaching to myself here—I once told my husband, in a fit of pregnancy-hormone rage, that the only reason I married him was so I'd have someone to kill the spiders). I realize we can swing too far to the opposite extreme and be scared to voice our opinions for fear of offending someone, but judging by the five o'clock news every night, the latter is not that big of a problem.

Your social media should be a reflection of who you are, so I'm not saying you should pretend to be someone else. But like a conversation, the purpose of social media is to communicate with others, which means it's not just about expressing yourself, it's also about who you are expressing yourself to. How do you balance those two things? Let's start with a short and easy quiz to see what your online habits might be saying about you.

### Social Media Personality Quiz

1. Your friend tags you in a photo in which she looks fabulous, but you think you look a little rough. What do you do?

    a. Send your friend a message telling her to take down the photo. ASAP!

    b. Untag yourself and then run and tell everyone that said girl is deliberately posting pictures of people who look worse than her.

    c. Untag yourself and send her an e-mail explaining that you loved that party and she looks fab, but you're untagging yourself because you're not a fan of how you look.

    d. Don't do anything. You'd rather just live with the photo than risk upsetting her.

2. You suddenly realize someone you thought was a good friend has deleted you from her friends list. What do you do?

   a. Ask her why she unfriended you. "Is it because I bought that same skirt? Why do you hate me?!?"

   b. Pretend you didn't notice while asking mutual friends if they know why.

   c. Mention to your friend that you noticed she's not on your friends list, and ask if she's having a problem with her account.

   d. Nothing. You assume she just doesn't want to be friends anymore.

3. You have a friend who posts way too many photos, of Every. Little. Thing. What do you do?

   a. Tell her no one cares that much about the pancakes she had for breakfast, or the sandals she found on sale, and she should do everyone a favor and *just stop posting so much*!

   b. Block her posts so you don't have to see them, and then discuss how ridiculous she is with your friends.

   c. Tolerate it, and comment occasionally if you actually like what she posted.

   d. Acknowledge every post. You may be annoyed, but you also want to be a supportive friend.

4. You find out your best friend is being bullied online. She tells you in confidence and says she doesn't want you to do anything because it will make things worse. What do you do?

a. Confront the people bullying her. If they mess with her, they're going to have to deal with you.

b. Write a passive-aggressive post about the situation, without naming names, but noting "You know who you are."

c. Respect your friend's request not to get involved but make a point of spending more time with her and encourage her to talk to others who may be able to help.

d. Tell her to ignore them, and respect her request to do nothing.

5. You're preparing for an interview for a job you really want when you realize some of the photos you and your friends have posted online might show you partying a bit too much. What do you do?

a. Nothing. Who cares if they see it? If they want to hire you, they can hire the *real* you.

b. Quickly go online and try to hide the worst ones from public view, and call all your friends and tell them to take down any/all risqué pics of you, too.

c. Sign off all your accounts to see what they'd be able to see. Then make sure any questionable photos are visible only to you and your friends. And keep them that way.

d. Just delete all photos from your account that don't make you look professional. Better to be safe than sorry.

**If you answered mostly A's:** You're bold, you're brash, and you tell it like it is! Your honesty and humor are strengths, but putting some restraints on what you say and what you post can only help you. When it comes to the Internet, tact and caution are your best friends! You will never regret saying too little, but you might regret saying too much.

**If you answered mostly B's:** You're a social butterfly and you've got tons of friends! That can be an asset in real life and online. However, learning to go straight to the source will help you deflect future conflicts. There's no sense in revving up the rumor mill when you can snuff out an argument at the start.

**If you answered mostly C's:** You're smart and well-liked by everyone! You try to exercise thought and caution with your dealings online. You're a friend to all, and that goes for your social media life, too. Just remember, you don't have to say yes to everyone all the time. In real life *or* online. Your time is valuable, so keep some for yourself.

**If you answered mostly D's:** You're thoughtful and sweet, and you just want to get along with everyone! Your easygoing nature and laid-back personality make you pleasant and easy to be around. Just don't let yourself become a doormat or be afraid to show your true colors—it's okay to show off your talents and sense of humor! If people don't like you, it's ultimately their problem, not yours.

Now that you have an idea of your social media personality, how can etiquette help you get where you're going? It's no secret that employers, bosses, and potential bosses are checking social media. Your page is your first impression, and you might not want your first impression to be tales of your debaucherous midnight snack run to Piggly Wiggly! On the other hand, a properly informed page can help you land your dream job or even forge a never-before-heard-of career.

Participating in social media is also an incredible way to meet people, including your *significant other* (cue the theatrical orchestra version of Canon in D), and to form a host of other potentially life-changing relationships (think LinkedIn). You can build a business, plan a trip, start a campaign, or fund a project. You could launch an online jewelry shop, create a custom artwork piece for your friend's wedding, or publish your own book. So, despite all of its pitfalls and shortcomings, I would argue that the online world has more stories of redemption and hope than anything else; more successes than failures. Many times, we hear only the horror stories and sad news; but, day in and day out, little victories are being won, goals are being reached, and people's lives are being changed all over the world because of something they saw, heard, or interacted with online. It would appear that social media, when done right, can lead to some pretty amazing things.

Singer/songwriter Rory Feek, of the former country music duo Joey + Rory, has endured unbelievable tests and trials (check out his blog, *This Life I Live*—but be prepared, you'll need a box of Kleenex) and yet remains hopeful and positive about life, love, and, yes, even the Internet. When his beloved wife, Joey, passed away from cancer, he found himself the recipient of countless thoughts, prayers, and condolences—all from complete strangers, as he had documented their story online. He says, "Sometimes I think the internet is a big scary place. A place where only dark things happen and the worst people in life get lifted up. But I don't think that way anymore. I think the internet is also a place where people can come together and share their hopes and their fears. A great big beautiful community of strangers...a great big, small town."[3]

How, then, do we dial it back and live a happy, healthy online existence? I think the answer lies in the question itself— the topic of social media *etiquette* has to return to its roots: etiquette. I am by no means Emily Post—in fact, I would probably fail at performing a proper cotillion. I've tripped down the steps in a filled-to-capacity auditorium, had a crucial button pop off my shirt seconds before a big event, and unknowingly lit a napkin on fire over dinner. Nevertheless, I love the thoughtfulness and tradition behind etiquette. My editor and I were discussing the origins of it one day over lunch when she proceeded to recount this fascinating table manners custom— dating back to early nineteenth-century dinner parties. I know it sounds a little ho-hum, but hang with me for a second—I promise it will be worth it.

Centuries ago, when etiquette was alive and well (we're

talking the Jane Austen era, folks), there was a customary rule that at formal dinners the host and hostess would sit at opposite ends of the table, with their guests lining the sides. When the first course was served, the ladies would turn to the right and talk to the gentleman who was seated directly to their right. When the next course was served, they would switch (aka "turn the table"), and each lady would turn and talk to the person on her left.[4] This was to avoid awkward conversations from happening across the table, with only some members of the dinner party engaged in the conversation and others feeling left out. The goal was for each person to have someone to talk to—for each person to feel welcomed and included. The spirit of the custom was in sheer consideration for the guests. That is the heart of most etiquette, my editor insists.

If we would view our social media pages and profiles in that light, I think life would be a lot easier and more pleasant online. Imagine yourself as the hostess and your page as your house. Everyone who visits is a guest, and it's your main job to make them feel comfortable, safe, and at home. Will they leave full and happy, or tired and cranky? Will they want to come back to your house (your page/profile) again? Let's all try to be good hostesses (myself included—the last time we had people over, I didn't serve the chips in a bowl; rather, I just threw the bag on the table. My mother was horrified).

If you need a few tips on how to become the quintessential social media hostess, just remember the four W questions.

## Who?

📰 Before you put something on the Internet, think about who will be able to see it. Your grandfather? Your friend who didn't get invited to the party? Your little sister and her friends? Potential employers? Sketchy Internet stalker? When in doubt, consider: Would you say this/show this to each of those people in person?

📰 Some platforms allow you to limit the audience, while others are very public. Beyond the image of yourself you're putting out there, know what's age appropriate and what's not. There are tons of kids online these days, so just remember that anything you say or do could very well be viewed by an eight-year-old.

## Why?

📰 There's nothing wrong with sharing that you're having a good time. Your one-year anniversary is definitely cause for celebration, and your elation/frustration with your new puppy's first mess on the floor is certainly good fodder for Facebook. You want people to feel engaged with what's going on in your life, and that's a good thing. But remember to ask yourself, *Am I sharing or showing off?*

📰 Are you reacting to something that upset you? Do you think that passive-aggressive tweet aimed at your friend is going to fix the situation? Before posting an angry message, wait at least an hour, sleep on it if you have to, and then decide if it will ultimately benefit or help someone.

## What?

📧 You want to present the best possible you online. Potential employers and family members might not want to see every pic from last night's shenanigans. Just try to remember that every image you post online could remain there forever. I'm not saying you need to airbrush every snapshot; simply use discretion when posting pictures.

📧 Don't alienate friends and readers with polarizing material. They're called "friends" for a reason—if it's a topic you wouldn't feel comfortable bringing up at a baby shower or a dinner party, it's probably not appropriate for an online audience either. Don't make them delete you!

📧 Will that rant incite an argument or a small online riot? If so, consider changing your words or simply not posting anything at all. If it's truly something vexing, then take it up directly with the offending party (I've done this wrong so many times, just take my word for it), or simply save a draft of it and, later, delete it. It's kind of a modern version of "Write an angry letter and throw it away."

## When?

📧 Because social media is always about what's happening right now, there's a tendency to share without thinking.

You also may find you're so busy updating your status that you're not fully appreciating the experience. It never hurts to wait a few hours—not every post needs to be written in the present tense. Try another tense:

- **Past:** "We had the best time at the Katy Perry concert last night [insert tags/photos of you all looking fabulous/inside joke here]!"
- **Imperfect:** "Even though it was raining, my nephew had so much fun at his birthday party. How cute is this video? (Yes, that's me as Chewbacca.)"

If you're at work, be sparing in your status updates. Most daily observations and commentary can wait until 5 p.m. to be posted. Coworkers online can see your profile, and even if they're not your Facebook friends, they'll notice if your screen is always filled with your feed. You don't want to give the impression that you're not pulling your own weight around the office.

Most people simply don't have time to scroll through countless stories and posts each day. There is so much proverbial noise in this world anyway; it's best to save lengthy anecdotes for an in-person conversation with a friend. Think of your online account as a highlight reel rather than a play-by-play.

At the end of the day, I don't think it's a matter of how much time you spend online or which picture you use for your profile; I don't think it's about the number of friends you have or even the percentage of retweets you get; I think it's your *reaction* to everything online that matters. The bad stuff—hurtful comments or a nasty message—shouldn't make you feel any worse about yourself, and the good stuff—Likes! Posts! Tweets!—shouldn't make you feel any better. Just be you. The rest of it—good or bad—doesn't really matter.

You see, social media was never meant to define us or label us or give us a sense of worth. It was meant to be a tool for communication—and by tool, I mean *one* tool—not the whole toolbox. There are still hundreds of other ways to express yourself, see the world, and experience life—outside of social media. You're not limited by your friends, your surroundings, or even your upbringing—and you're certainly not limited by what your profile says. There's more to you than the 140 characters you can fit into a tweet. A twenty-word bio could never do you justice. Life is bigger than your friends list or your Instagram account. You were perfectly you before you had a Facebook account, and you'll be perfectly you after you get sick of Snapchat. The message is: Don't let online images, messages, gossip, or news get to you—just smile and hold your head high (that might be the only way you'll get off your phone ☺)!

## Chapter Three

# Just a Little Bit (of Respect)

"Don't lower your standards for anyone or anything.
Self-respect is everything." —*Anonymous*

In the eternal voice of Mama Aretha: "R-E-S-P-E-C-T!" Besides being a flat-out brilliant song, the message is still clear and relevant forty-some years after its release date. Aretha figured out what it meant, and we can too. Self-respect is one of the greatest assets a girl can possess. It's an elusive noun, though—what does *self-respect* mean? What does it look like? I think it's knowing that you're worth it, and then acting like it. Knowing that you're worth being treated with kindness and value. It's loving yourself and not needing anyone else to complete you. I'll be honest, I kind of like myself. I enjoy hanging out with me, because, well, I think I'm fun. If that were the long and the short of it, it might be easy, but self-respect is more than just having the ability to crack yourself up. It's about how you relate to other people, how others relate to you, and, ultimately, the legacy you leave after you're gone.

One of the fastest ways to gain (or lose) respect is with

your image. Adele looks fierce and fabulous when taking the main stage in her signature floor-length gowns. When Ivanka Trump conducts business meetings in classy designer duds she looks intelligent and capable. Though we're no longer living in Audrey's bygone era of pearls, full skirts, and record players, the possession of elusive qualities like poise and grace is still in style. Before we even open our mouths to speak, our clothes will always do the talking for us, announcing loudly whether or not we respect ourselves. It's true that you never get a second chance to make a first impression, and many of our first impressions are crucial ones—interviewing for a big job, meeting future in-laws, making an important business contact, going on a blind date. The first impression should be memorable...in a good way.

We rarely hear about someone being judged for covering up too much skin, but the minute a star steps out in a see-through, low-cut dress, we read about it in the next day's headlines. Wardrobe triumphs and taboos are always points for conversation, and when things are too tight or too small, when tops are loosed and bottoms are exposed, rest assured that people are going to talk. And in this case, it's best to be on the receiving end of flattering remarks and glowing compliments rather than getting the short end of the apparel stick. When in doubt about an outfit, err on the side of caution. People would be hard-pressed to find something bad to say when you look modestly glamorous.

Is your image leaving you feeling confident? Are your

actions speaking volumes of your confidence and self-respect? Take this quick quiz to find out!

## Guide to Self-Respect Quiz

1. It's girls' night out, and you're doing dinner and a movie. You:
    a. Change into some flattering jeans and a cute new top.
    b. Slip on your va-va-voom dress—you never know where the night will lead!
    c. Pull on your comfy clothes; your friends won't care.
2. While you're waiting in the lobby for your big interview, you:
    a. Review the latest post on the company's blog on your phone and try to sit up straight.
    b. Make a beeline for the bathroom to apply more lipstick.
    c. Become engrossed in the novel you brought.
3. After a successful first date with sweet, handsome has-to-be-The-One, you:
    a. Settle for one good-night kiss and wait for him to call.
    b. Flood his phone with texts, hearts, and googly-eyed emojis.
    c. Figure he's out of your league and down a pint of Ben & Jerry's.
4. When asked to take part in something inappropriate during sorority rush week, you:

    a. Politely decline and spend the night studying for your big exam.

    b. Don't ask questions; just hop in the car to get to said location!

    c. Go along with the group, even though you feel a bit uncomfortable.

5. You're at a dance with friends and realize you've had a wardrobe malfunction. You:

    a. Run to the bathroom to see if your dress can be salvaged with some safety pins.

    b. Keep dancing. Who cares who sees what?

    c. Sprint to your car and grab a sweatshirt to cover up.

Now tally up the letters. What's your answer?

**If you picked mostly A's:** You are thoughtful and classy. You have lots of positive role models in your life, and you work to be one yourself. You know how to work what you've got but never flaunt it to the point of excess. Stylewise, you're trendy but not a slave to fashion, and you exude confidence wherever you go. Friends look to you for advice, and guys respect you for respecting yourself. Occasionally, people might mistake your confidence for arrogance, though. Just don't forget to let down your guard every once in a while and be open to off-the-beaten-path options in style, life, and love (nerd glasses, a goofy boyfriend—you get the idea).

**If you picked mostly B's:** You live life out loud! You're not afraid to be yourself anytime, anywhere. Whether at work, home, or school, you're usually the center of attention. You're fun, crazy, and the life of the party—you're never one to shy away from drama, conflict, or confrontation. Stylewise, the top of your closet is full of tops and dresses that are as bold as you are; the bottom of your closet is littered with heels, tanks, and a few bras with broken straps. Your friends are your life and they know all your secrets—good, bad, and ugly. Guys might be intimidated by your bold style, so go easy on them. Just don't forget to keep a few classics on hand (a well-fitting black dress for formal events, a demure jacket for chilly date nights), and a polished résumé for job interviews.

**If you picked mostly C's:** You're easygoing and a welcome addition to any group! You're smart, thoughtful, and always concerned with other people's feelings. You're easy to be around because you're a friend to everyone. Stylewise, you like to be comfortable. If a new fashion item pinches, squeezes, or bunches, then it's not for you. Friends love to have you around because you're a good listener and fiercely loyal. Guys find you attractive and approachable due to your laid-back nature. Don't be afraid to step out of your comfort zone every once in a while and try something new—even if it's just a new food (kale?) or pair of shoes (gladiator sandals?). You might be pleasantly surprised.

Thanks to the fact that we're diverse, the smart, sophisticated girl-world is going to look a little different to each of us; we wouldn't want it any other way. Not one of us is going to look exactly like Audrey Hepburn, and that's just fine. We can pursue class, style, and grace in our own distinct ways, no matter where we fall on the classy/graceful/stylish spectrum.

The great thing about self-respect is that it has nothing to do with wealth. Being classy is an attitude and outlook on life; the art of gracefulness is how we behave and act when no one is watching; being stylish is how we present ourselves to others. It might involve our clothes, but it's not defined by designer labels. It might include our jobs, but it doesn't matter if we are white-collar or blue-collar. It might entail a different set of social obligations, but it's not dictated by where we were raised. Why? *Because class is not defined by our circumstances—it's our reaction to those circumstances that defines who we are.* It doesn't matter if you work at McDonald's or the White House—are you punctual and courteous? It is not a matter of whether you went to an exclusive private institution or a tuition-free public school—did you make the most of every opportunity given to you? It doesn't make a bit of difference whether you're designing clothes for Vera Wang or working in the fabric section of Walmart—are you attentive and accommodating? No matter what your upbringing was, what your current friend situation looks like, or what your yearly income is, you can possess poise and self-respect. You can be stylish and classy no matter where you are, who you know, or what you do.

One of the greatest benefits of living with confidence and self-worth is that we don't need to constantly rely on others for fulfillment. People are always going to have their opinions and judgments, so don't let their petty commentary affect who you are. And who you are is unique! When you know who you are, you no longer have to sport the teensiest tops for attention, get high to have fun, or let the first guy who asks you out decide how physical things get. When you naturally feel good about yourself, you can focus on being the fabulous female you are, rather than seeking approval from every Tom, Dick, and Harry. It's a freeing mind-set to no longer have to derive our value from others.

How do you start implementing a modern yet old-fashioned level of self-respect in your life? Don't settle for others' compliments or rely solely on outside influences—you've got to start by loving yourself. If you didn't have perfect parents or the greatest upbringing, you can still respect yourself. Perhaps your friends have been less than supportive—no worries, you can still love yourself. And as much as we are trained to believe that guys will bring fulfillment to our lives, they won't bring everlasting happiness either. We won't find it in short skirts or catcalls or lap dances or one-night stands—it has to start with us. If you don't respect yourself, no one else will.

One of the best ways to cultivate a healthy self-image is by celebrating your positive and unique qualities. Try a few of the following exercises to further confirm your lovely, distinct traits and characteristics.

👆 **Make a list of loves.** Think about things you love to do and why. What qualities that you possess make you passionate about those things? Make a list of the things that make you *you* and post it someplace where you'll see it daily.

👍 **See yourself in them.** List the characteristics of someone you admire, whether it be an actress or your grandma. Which of those characteristics do you see in yourself? What goals do you share? What areas do you want to improve on?

👍 **Find your niche.** What do you have to give the world that no one else can? At the risk of sounding like a hokey self-help guru, I am convinced that every person has a unique set of gifts specifically designed to contribute to the world, and if those gifts aren't used, a void will go unfilled. You'll never know what an impact you could make until you try.

👍 **Get a second opinion.** Ask a close friend or family member what they think are some of your most unique gifts and traits. Sometimes outside parties can see us better than we can see ourselves. I think these were called "warm fuzzies" in elementary school.

👍 **Get out.** One of the best ways to instantly boost your mood and self-image is to get a little fresh air. Especially if you're experiencing the day-in-and-day-out drain of fluorescent office lighting, just half an hour of natural sunlight will do wonders for a sagging attitude. Walk to your lunch spot, or simply stroll around the block during your break.

👍 **Educate yourself.** The more you know, the better you feel about yourself. Get informed on political issues, global needs, current events, and even new books and movies, and feel your knowledge expand.

👍 **Try something new.** Discover a new skill, talent, or interest by doing something you've never done before. Visit a museum, attend a local event, or try out a new hobby, maybe Geocaching or watercolor painting (I think one of the greatest advantages of modern society is our access and proximity, at any given moment, to a BYOB painting class).

👍 **Give it away.** Do something nice for someone else. Surprise a pregnant coworker with a baby gift, help an elderly neighbor take out the trash, take your mom on a lunch date—nothing will boost your self-confidence more quickly than a random act of kindness.

Now that we're committed to putting self-respect first, what's the next step? As we determined before, our outward appearance makes the first and strongest impression, so let's go there.

First things first: Consider the context. I'm all for wearing what makes you feel good, but it's a good rule of thumb to consider the nature of the event you're attending. A family wedding, a sister's twenty-first birthday party, or the funeral of a close friend—almost every occasion has an unspoken dress code. And while I sympathize with the "Girls Rock!" sentiment to dress however you want and let the chips fall where they may, I also agree that it's in good taste to be considerate of those around you. In short, it all goes back to our definition of etiquette—does what you're wearing make those around you feel uncomfortable or put them at ease? Does your ensemble make others calm or nervous? Even though you may have the bod to rock booty shorts during your flight to Las Vegas, it might make the family of five behind you in line uncomfortable. Does your office have an unspoken business-casual dress code? Then a tight spaghetti-strap tank might be a distraction to your married, forty-something male coworker. It's all about taking the feelings of the people around you into consideration.

Next, behold the power of good posture (my mom's famous last words before I have any public appearance are always "Just be yourself, and sit up straight!"). Standing up straight instantly inspires respect and gets attention. You won't believe what good posture will do for your image (even five-foot-eleven Nicole Kidman stands tall while walking the red carpet). So pull those shoulders back and hold your head up high. You'll feel like you've undergone an instant makeover, and you'll look like it, too—great posture can make you instantly appear five pounds slimmer. And not only will you *appear* more confident, but you'll *feel* more confident.

To make things easier, when you leave the house each morning, make a mental note to walk taller (or leave yourself an actual note on the door). Then try replacing that stiff executive desk chair at the office or at home with a core-strengthening, posture-improving exercise ball (I recommend the Gaiam Balance Ball Chair—it's available in different colors). Then sign up for a Pilates class with a girlfriend, and within a week you'll feel inches taller and be gliding along the sidewalks like Gwyneth Paltrow. Add a two-inch heel, and you may well be truly unstoppable.

Last but not least, work on making eye contact. It's just a tiny detail, but it could make the difference between being just another shifty-eyed shrinking violet and getting that big job. I still remember what the woman told me during my first-ever job interview when I was fourteen—I was applying to work at a little bookstore in the mall and she ended the interview by saying, "You can relax, you got the job. But in the future, remember to make eye contact." I was utterly terrified, so I robotically shook my head yes and vowed to take her words to heart.

Fast-forward a few years—living in Nashville and working in the music industry, I conducted lots of media-training sessions with artists and bands, and one of the first rules of thumb taught is to maintain eye contact with the interviewer or audience. I have personally seen the positive effects of eye contact—it can make the difference between a good review or a bad one. My sweet friend singer/songwriter Meredith Andrews is the best at this—she's so engaged and attentive and makes interviewers and fans truly feel special when she's talking to them. Of her supernatural ability to create an atmosphere of acceptance and value she says, "I count it a privilege to speak into the lives of others, whether from the stage or on an individual basis, so I want to make that person feel like he or she is the only one in the room. My goal," she adds, "is to maintain accessibility and honesty."

Good eye contact personally connects you with your audience and cuts physical distance in half, so make it a point to lock eyeballs with friends when they're talking, with dates over dinner, and with your boss while he's giving you an assignment. Whether you're at an interview or a cocktail party, eye contact with fellow conversers will communicate intelligence and aplomb. Not only will you appear more personable, you'll have an instant air of confidence and self-possession. Confident girls who conduct themselves with style and grace are memorable, and when you make eye contact with those around you, you'll be hard to forget.

Our current shopaholic/clubaholic/talkaholic culture is very different from our grandmothers' world of sock hops and petticoats. It can take years to build trust and gain respect from others, and those gains can be lost entirely with just one bad move. Between all of the promises from get-famous-quick schemes and the instantaneous nature of video-sharing, it's easy to do some irreparable damage with just one lax step. It can make you a little crazy thinking of all the possible ways to *lose* your reputation before you've even had a chance to build a good one. So rather than focusing on what not to do (I think we all know the taboo subjects to be avoided), let's set our minds on the best ways to *build* a good reputation. How do we do that? I personally believe that self-respect stems from discipline, and discipline is all about the little (and big) choices we make every day. And the big ones might not be as difficult to make as you think.

First of all, we simply need to ask ourselves what we would do if our grandmothers were here. Would Grandma approve of that audition tape for _____ (insert your own favorite reality show)? How about the boy you're currently seeing? Or how about a tabletop birthday dance? It's a humbling and horrifying thing to discover that someone is always watching. It makes you look at everything with new eyes. An impressionable niece, a grandparent, a boss, or just a friend who looks up to you might be affected by your actions. You possess more power than you know! You can make the difference in someone's life, so use that opportunity for the better. Speak into someone's life and encourage them to pursue their dreams. The people in your life are there for a reason. After years of building our reputations as hard workers, intelligent students, and the world's greatest daughters, why would we want to throw it all away on one impulsive moment? Stay strong.

No opportunity is so worthwhile, no circumstance so urgent, that we should ditch our values and convictions. It may be tempting to text that sultry selfie to the guy you like, but will you be okay with him forwarding it to all his friends? And while it can be tons of fun to go see a show until the wee hours on a Wednesday, does your job depend on your being on time in the morning? (Some of my poorer college grades were a direct result of my making it a priority to be at every show at a local music venue called Exit/In—at least I grew musically that semester, if not academically.) Whatever you decide, just be sure to set your standards high and stick by them no matter what.

Now, we're respectable dames, but that doesn't mean we can't have any fun. Call them what you will—do-gooders, prudes, goody two-shoes (do people still use that term?)—the quintessential good girls always get a bad rap for being dull, priggish, lame, and stuffy. But I've got a lot of friends who could give Melissa McCarthy and Kristen Wiig a run for their comedic money. Just because our idea of a good time isn't the same as someone else's doesn't mean it's any less fun. Life is what you make it—so if you want to be smart and have fun, then be smart and have fun. Don't let anybody make you feel like less of a person just because you don't want to partake in what you consider questionable activities. Just be you and hold your head high. In celebration of our tasteful craziness, I've listed a few (tried-and-tested) classy, graceful, and stylish alternatives that will solidify your It Girl status yet leave you feeling regret-free the next day:

1. The next time the gang goes out for the night, try springing for a virgin Bellini instead of the usual martini. I know it's hard to be the one lone wolf in the party who's

not drinking (if I had a nickel for every time someone has said, "Are you *pregnant*? Is *that* why you're not drinking?"), so come prepared with your own nonalcoholic drink order. This is one of my favorites (my husband used to be a bartender, so I've made him fix me every yummy nonalcoholic concoction in the book). This sweet, peachy/beachy drink is fun, tasty, and pretty to look at. But best of all, you'll remember how you got home. Try it during your next night out, and even if the girls are coming over for a fun night in, whip up the quick, easy recipe at home.

### *Virgin Bellini*

*1 part peach syrup*
*3 parts Sprite*
*Ice cubes*
*Dash of cherry grenadine*
*Maraschino cherries (optional)*

1. Pour the peach syrup and Sprite into a blender with ice that is equivalent to the liquid level. Blend.

2. Pour into tall champagne flutes and add a dash of cherry grenadine for flavor and color.

3. Serve with maraschino cherries (optional). Bottoms up!

2. If you're bored with celebrity gossip or tired of ho-hum entertainment, break out of your rut and tackle a fun DIY

project for your apartment or dorm room. Surf Pinterest for ideas and inspiration, then scout out local yard sales, flea markets, or Goodwill for unique pieces. My husband and I love to go to auctions and estate sales (that's only mildly creepy, right?), because you never know what you might find. You could turn an old milk crate into a storage box for magazines, glue a bunch of used books together for a cool centerpiece, or refinish an old bureau with chalkboard paint. When in doubt, simply ask yourself, "WWJGD?" (What Would Joanna Gaines Do?)

3. If you're like me, your phone is just one big flurry of multitasking goings-on—usually something more akin to *Let's Make a Deal* than a well-organized system of checks and balances. Behind Door Number One we're... shopping for new spring break shorts! Behind Door Number Two... we're typing an e-mail to our boss! Behind Door Number Three we're... trying to figure out the payback for our student loan! *Wohn wohn wohhhhn.* Rather than updating your Facebook status, head on over to your e-mail account and type up a quick message to your best friend from high school whom you haven't said boo to in ages. Chances are you have stuff to catch up on, and it will make her or his day to hear from you.

4. Have you recently been contacted by a less-than-reputable male (a person you would usually never give a second thought to, but you're lonely)? Don't let yourself give in to desperation! I know singledom can sometimes make

you feel isolated, but there's nothing wrong with being single—you should never feel that you have to be in a relationship to be a complete person. If you happen to want a relationship, remember that just because you're not with someone right now doesn't mean you won't be in the very near future. You never know when, or where, love might find you. So don't feel as if you have go out with just any guy because you feel sorry for him or for yourself. There is no reason whatsoever for someone as classy and fabulous as you to stoop to desperate lows just because you're beginning to feel like a loner. Rather than lowering your standards and settling for someone, show him the door and go buy that great pair of boots you've been wanting (feel free to sing "R-E-S-P-E-C-T" on the way to the store).

5. It can be disheartening when it appears as though every normal young lady now has the body of a Greek goddess. Through plastic surgery, implants, and Botox, we can manipulate our bodies to do just about anything we want them to. The question is, do you want to live with it forever? Some procedures are irreversible, and in ten years you may not feel the same way about your nose, cheeks, or, ahem, chest region. When those of us who *have* stuck with what nature gave us start to feel like chopped liver, certain options can begin to be appealing. If you're looking for alternative options with the same feel-good result, consider spending those hard-earned dollars on

a cruise to the Bahamas rather than blowing all your savings on a shoddy enhancement job. Or surprise your sister with a weekend getaway at a luxury spa. You'll have great memories and still be au naturel.

If we think that we are the only ones who benefit from our classy choices, we're wrong. Reese Witherspoon recently launched her own chic, Southern-flavored clothing line, Draper James, and had this to say about the importance of intelligence and respect: "Creating a cultural icon out of someone who goes, 'I'm stupid, isn't it cute?' makes me want to throw daggers. I want to say to them, 'My grandma did not fight for what she fought for just so you can start telling women it's fun to be stupid. Saying that to young women, little girls, my daughter? It's not okay.'"[5] Self-respect isn't just for us, for the now. It's also for the preservation of the dignity, class, and fabulousness of femininity for future generations of young women.

It's hard to think of the legacy you want to leave when you're in the heat of the moment—it's difficult to remember what you want to be remembered for when you're being faced with a choice in the here and now. Suddenly the faces of the sister who looks up to you and your proud dad are hard to imagine when you're being cornered about an issue. I've found that it's easier if you already know, before you even get into the sticky situation, what you're going to do or say. So make up your mind beforehand. Then circumstances won't take you by surprise. No matter what you're faced with, you'll already know your answer and be able to deliver it with strength and conviction. It'll save you from floundering when you're being confronted; it takes the waffling out of a peer pressure situation. Here's what you do. Write down a list of three things you *will* do in your life (goals you want to accomplish; dreams you want to see fulfilled) and three things you *won't* do (values that are nonnegotiable; things you won't compromise on). When in doubt about your own values and beliefs, consult the list that you made—check out the standards that you set for yourself!

---

### 3 Things I *Will* Do

_____

_____

_____

### 3 Things I *Won't* Do

_____

_____

_____

If the personal benefits of self-respect aren't initiative enough to up the class factor, then the lure of a potential boyfriend will sometimes do the trick. While it appears that sometimes guys can't see past the short skirt in front of them, men (read: the ones who are worth your time) are more perceptive than we give them credit for. Would an average red-blooded male rather have a self-respecting girl than anything else? Survey says: Yes!

Most of us have been tricked into thinking that most men are simply in it for the carnal aspects of a relationship, but you might be surprised to find that the majority of guys have more in mind than just patches of exposed skin. Even though most guys haven't been planning their weddings since second grade (I had a "wedding book" in kindergarten, complete with cut-out pictures of my future cake and bridesmaids' dresses; my husband said his childhood days were consumed with little more than thoughts of dump trucks and Kirby Puckett), they still have forever on their brain. How do I know? Because not every love song was written by a female, that's why. Plenty of male artists and songwriters have written countless homages dedicated to the subject of finding their soul mate. We're not the only ones who dream about finding "the one" and settling down with 2.5 kids and a nice picket fence.

Though it may not seem like it at times, many guys prefer a smart, self-respecting girl they could take home to their moms. One of my close guy friends even told me, "Most guys aren't actually interested in cheap girls." He went on to disclose that while they might be "fun for a while," they will probably never make it home to Mom, because guys ultimately want an interesting girl who can hold an intelligent conversation.

Out of curiosity, I posed the question to several other guy friends and coworkers in a casual, informal environment (and was certifiably shocked by my findings). I asked, "When given the choice, would you prefer a girl who is simply nice to look at, or one you could take home to your mom?" To my pleasant surprise, *every one of them* said they would prefer the girl next door. It was not only gratifying to hear but renewed my faith in the male gender. Bravo, boys! In conclusion, my rudimentary research tells me that if we want their undivided attention for about 2.4 seconds, we should bust out a glitter mini and do the bend-and-snap. But if we want a real relationship with a real gentleman, we should just keep being our smart, classy, fabulous selves and they'll be beating down our doors in no time.

But what about those few bad seeds who are in it just for a one-night stand? Well, I don't know about you, but I personally wouldn't want to be with a guy who doesn't respect me, let alone care if I respect myself. He is obviously not worth your time. If you're feeling pressured to go further than you're comfortable with, here's a good note to keep in mind: *If they don't want us without the physical stuff, they're not going to want us with it.* Feel free to tape that to your bathroom mirror and read it every morning. If a guy is not really into you before hooking up, then going all the way is not going to change anything. You are worth way too much to give away pieces of yourself to someone who doesn't love or respect you. And if he's saying he loves you and is *still* trying to get you to push the envelope, then I'm sorry to say it's not love. Save yourself for someone who believes the same way you do. You won't regret it.

If there's one thing that we intelligent, beautiful, and funnier-than-heck girls are *not*, it is desperate. A self-respecting girl doesn't need a piece of arm candy to walk tall or a partner to make her life complete. No woman should ever have to convince a guy to want to be with her—*ever*. If a guy isn't into you, it's his loss. Cut him loose and move on already. Sure, I've blubbered for a few days over a lost love, but I do not advocate crying into bowls of Ben & Jerry's for months over a rejection that came from someone else—any guy who has driven you to that point isn't worth your precious time, emotions, or Kleenex.

So you've been doing everything a good, modern, old-fashioned girl should—holding your head high, exuding style and poise with intelligence and confidence—and you have yet to land your dream job. You have yet to meet Mr. Right. You're not even sure you'll get into grad school. Does it ever feel like it's just too hard? Does it seem like everyone else is getting ahead (even while *they're* not making good choices)? Is it really worth it to work hard, live with integrity, and maintain your

self-worth? Is there a payoff for walking the straight and nar-
row? When you're fourteen, it doesn't look like it. But by the
time you get to twenty-two, twenty-eight, thirty-five, you'll be
glad you did. And sometimes, you need a good old-fashioned
success story to keep you going.

I'm kind of in love with this professional snowboarder
named Kelly Clark. She went to her first Olympics at age eigh-
teen. She says, "When it's rough going, I think about what is
happening instead of what's not happening: something, even
if it's small, is always going right, and you're always getting
better at something."[6] Her hard work has paid off—Kelly is
now a *four-time* Olympian and the most decorated half-pipe
snowboarder in the sport's history. She's even started a foundation to empower youth and young snowboarders—helping
them turn their dreams into realty through scholarships,
resources, and opportunities.

Another Olympian, gymnast Gabby Douglas, was the first
African American to win the individual all-around event at the
2012 Summer Games. But she had to leave her family and her
home at an early age to train, and she inevitably missed them
dearly. Winning a gold medal at the Olympics made it all
worthwhile, though, and the history-making young woman
has said, "My mom definitely inspired me every single day...
she taught me in life, to always keep fighting, and nothing is
handed to you directly. So you just always have to fight for it."[7]

My friends, that's what it is all about: being comfortable in
your own skin. So many of us waste so much of our lives trying

to fit into someone else's life—someone else's definition of happy. The truth is, there's only one you. No one's going to do things the same way as you. No one's going to enjoy the exact same things as you. And that's a good thing. Having good old-fashioned self-respect is undoubtedly a big stepping-stone on that bridge of happiness. Knowing that you're loved is a key to unlocking a lifetime of contentment. Why? Because when you feel good about yourself, you can be joyful in any situation—even if the situation is not ideal. You see, being happy is not about being naive or unrealistic, it's simply the ability to look at a situation and say to yourself, *I know what the facts are, but I'm going to hope for the best anyway.* Self-respect is exactly what it says: respect for yourself. No one else can muster it up for you, but the minute you begin to tap into it, others will immediately take note. One of the best things you can do for your future is to love and respect yourself.

## Chapter Four

# Words, Words, Words

"I think, with never-ending gratitude, that the young
women of today do not and can never know at what
price their right to free speech and to speak at all in
public has been earned." —*Lucy Stone*[8]

Great women like Susan B. Anthony, Sojourner Truth, and Anne Sullivan, who contributed so much to society and made so many advances for our nation and gender, might be rolling in their graves right now. The sheer number of "likes" and "whatevers" in my own daily speech is horrifying, not to mention the vulgarity and idiocy found in the average comments section of any Internet article. Our language is constantly changing and evolving, and has done so irreversibly since the days of *Pride and Prejudice*. I have a hard time getting through some classic literature as the language is almost unrecognizable, and I'm sure they would say the same about the majority of our lingo today. Sidenote: I have this idea for a reality show where you dig up old authors and dignitaries and make them take part in current TV shows. Tell me you wouldn't watch Sylvia Plath on *Shark Tank*, Shakespeare freestyling poetry on *Britain's*

*Got Talent*, or Tolstoy guest-starring on the new Kevin James sit-com. (I'm borderline in love with Kevin, so I had to squeeze him into this book somehow.) The language barrier between generations seems almost as big as the language barrier between countries. Nevertheless, our words still have the power to reach people, effect change, and make history.

Lucy Stone was right—we don't truly know the price paid by those who went before us. Things we take for granted on a daily basis—the freedom to shout out an answer in class, an unlimited number of career options, flippancy in registering to vote—were once considered impossibilities and nothing more than pipe dreams. But thanks to the blood, sweat, and tears of countless women throughout history, we have incredible privileges today, and I, for one, am very thankful.

I am truly in awe of people like Sacagawea and Laura Ingalls Wilder—these amazing women who went before us forded rivers, built cabins, and raised a generation of children with no self-help or parenting books. They made their own clothing, cooked meals from scratch, and educated themselves and their families. It makes me feel positively silly for complaining about "not knowing what to fix for dinner." Maybe they knew something we don't know? Were they aware of what a trail they were blazing? Pioneers, in any respect of the word, never have it easy. But the legacy they leave behind is crucial. Everything they fought for, died for, and lived for has been indispensable to the success of future generations. Although it seems hard to imagine, the truth is that we have that same potential to change the world; we have a voice and a life to be lived just as they did; it's just a matter of how we make ourselves heard.

How can we honor the past while still living (and talking) in the twenty-first century? I think it's much like our etiquette revelation—it's the heart of language that matters. Language is a tool for communication, and when used correctly, it can brighten someone's day, speak love to someone who's never known love, or even teach a child to read. And while at most times we are encouraged to speak up, state our opinions, or say what's on our minds, there can be just as great a power in not saying anything at all. Many times, the power of language lies in our ability to tame our tongues.

Whether or not we realize it, people are always listening and judging the words that come out of our mouths. Your boss could be just around the corner while you gab in the break room about your wild weekend. Your impressionable niece might pick up an ugly phrase or two while you're candidly talking on the phone to a friend. And that date on Saturday night might not be so charmed by your excessive usage of the f-bomb. All of these people (and more) are constantly making assumptions about our character based on our daily tête-à-têtes, our uncensored musings, and our friendly chitchat.

They say actions speak louder than words. That is true,

but one bad verbal slipup could mean the tarnishing of a hard-earned reputation. Don't freak yourself out, though—everyone makes mistakes. The best thing you can do is acknowledge the error, learn from the oops, and try harder next time. That's all any of us can do.

If you think that what we say doesn't matter, check out the following quote from an unknown source:

> *Watch your thoughts, for they become words.*
> *Watch your words, for they become actions.*
> *Watch your actions, for they become habits.*
> *Watch your habits, for they become character.*
> *Watch your character, for it becomes your destiny.*

So how do we begin to rein in our words and speak with poise and grace? It's no easy task, that's for sure. I've spouted enough garbage to personally enlarge a landfill. And the bad thing is, once it's out there, you can never get it back. The trick, therefore, is not to say the asinine thing in the first place. Which would seemingly require a lot of discipline. Not exactly the thing we're thinking of when conversing about the latest Bella Thorne flick or that cute guy from work. However, with a little self-discipline, we can learn to tame the tongue and speak wisdom, positivity, and love. And one of the best ways to break the verbal spin cycle is to get out of our cushy verbal comfort zone.

Start by finding people around you who inspire you—teachers, pastors, aunts, anyone. By surrounding yourself with people who are older and wiser, you'll be inspired and motivated to up the ante when it comes to your speech. I love hanging out with older friends and mentors because it's a good reminder that I still have so much to learn. I always leave thinking, *I need to read more, listen more, and pray more if I'm going to make it in this life.* You also probably find that you adapt your speech without thinking to fit the people you're with. So if you're tempted to slip back into your old ways, just imagine that your grandmother, or whomever you deeply respect, is standing behind you.

This may come as a shock to you but I'm kind of obsessed with learning and personal growth. Consequently, I'm always on the lookout for things that stimulate the brain, aka Smart Girl activities. To kick off our wordfest, take a crack at some of the following Smart Girl Do's to get yourself thinking (and talking) outside the box.

🖉 Do a crossword puzzle every day over your lunch break.

🖉 Pick up a learn-a-word-a-day desk calendar or app.

🖉 Check out a foreign language instructional program from your library or download a learn-a-new-language app and listen during your commute to work.

🖉 Play word games either online or with friends. My personal favorites are Scattergories, Catch Phrase, and Scrabble.

🖉 Record yourself talking—note any unnecessary or, like, filler words that you should, you know, maybe not use.

📎 Subscribe to a thought-provoking or inspirational podcast.

📎 Intersperse some nonfiction books throughout your usual *Glamour* fix and chick-lit routine.

📎 Read the dictionary during ads and commercials. That may sound extreme, but I actually used to read the dictionary for fun when I was little. Yes, I am *that* dorky.

One of my favorite novelists is George Eliot. I was halfway through a book report before I figured out that he was a she. Nevertheless, she wisely once said, "Blessed is the man who, having nothing to say, abstains from giving us wordy evidence of the fact."[9] I think it's human nature to feel the need to talk more, the less we know about something. I think it's an insecurity thing—to cover up for the fact that we're actually clueless. Truth be told, I can yammer on endlessly for hours about subjects on which I have no authority whatsoever. But history would tell us that almost everyone can talk; it's the people who actually have something to *say* who make the greatest difference.

Perhaps one of the most crucial aspects of learning to speak with authority and intelligence is being informed. Before there was Jimmy Fallon (whom I adore), there was Jay Leno and his famous segment called "Jaywalking," in which the comical host would hit the streets and quiz innocent passersby on everything from political issues to historical figures. Questions like "Who signed the Declaration of Independence?"

would be met with responses such as "Madonna?" or "Al Pacino?" Truthfully, it's almost always easy to laugh at people's ludicrous responses and lack of knowledge, but the fact is that I'm far from being well-versed on every current trend and issue. In fact, my husband asserts that most of my knowledge of twentieth-century events is completely derived from the song "We Didn't Start the Fire."

How do we become educated on the concerns facing our generation? Or begin to understand world events? It's somewhat of a daunting subject. I say, take it one step at a time. If the problems in the Middle East are too overwhelming, then start by looking into some local topics of concern. Find out what issues are being voted on at the next town council meeting. Volunteer to be part of a local campaign or nonprofit organization. Look for the need closest to you, then go help to meet that need. Being an informed and productive member of society needn't be complicated: It's a matter of simply taking thirty minutes to cast a ballot in each election. It means getting engaged with the needs of our city, county, nation, and world. It means discovering our own opinions, passions, and voice and using them to impact events around us.

I also believe that becoming an informed member of society means seeking out the right information, not just taking the information given to us at face value. Rather than blindly absorbing the thoughts and stories dictated by the news or media, think for yourself and work to unearth the truth in every situation. Rather than going along with our favorite celebrity's political endorsement, do some research and determine your own convictions on the issues. Instead of accepting mass media reports as reality, be willing to dig for the actual facts in each story. I actually think it's kind of fun to check things out and educate yourself—it gives you a sense of ownership: *This* is what I believe and *this* is the truth. It's powerful. My wise and witty seventh-grade civics teacher, Mr. Rock, had a poster hanging in his classroom that read:

> What's Popular Is Not Always Right,
> and What's Right Is Not Always Popular

I've always loved that. We can't assume that the current trend is always the best thing. I have a closet full of high-waisted jeans to prove that's true. Cultural values and rights are no different. Rather than taking them for granted, we need to become more informed and use our voices wisely. How do you achieve and maintain an informed mind? To keep from merely falling in line with society's group sentiments, it's important to educate yourself daily: Sign up for an unbiased political blog, set your laptop's home page to a daily headline source, or go old-school and subscribe to a newspaper. Okay, I'll admit, half of the info I hear consists of secondhand reports from my husband—he checks the news more than I do and, consequently, regularly informs me of anything new and noteworthy (although he's been instructed to deliberately edit out the gory parts and anything traumatizing that involves children). The point is, we can become involved in our local government, vote regularly, contribute to a think tank, or simply donate time and energy to a cause that means something to us. Great women of history put their lives on the line just so we could have the right to speak out and use our voices for good, so let's do them proud.

---

Looking for some extra motivation, or just in the mood for a night of ladylike camaraderie? Here are eight fun, female-centric movies to empower, inspire, and entertain:

- *Suffragette*
- *Bend It Like Beckham*
- *Julie & Julia*
- *A League of Their Own*
- *Whip It*
- *Blue Crush*
- *Frozen*
- *Bring It On*

---

When it comes to social graces and polite niceties, they sometimes appear to be a dying breed. Customs like bringing a gift for the hostess, or taking a meal to a friend in need, are likened to tales from days of yore. Compliments and genuine gratitude are seemingly bred into only a rare few, but perhaps that's a good thing; otherwise, reality shows would all but dry up due to a lack of drama and ridiculousness! I kid, I kid.

The truth is, I witness courteous actions and proper

etiquette on a daily basis, and I know you do, too. In the South, many boys are still taught to open doors for women, pull out chairs, and say "Yes, ma'am" and "No, sir." Many young women are still taught how to properly host a dinner party, how to decorate for the holidays, and how to make a mean batch of biscuits. I'll admit it—one of my favorite magazines is *Southern Living*. I'm not sure what the target demographic is, but I can't help myself—I love it. Manners aren't confined to the South, though; I've seen acts of kindness all around the country—from the New York City subway to the Pacific Coast Highway. Kindness is still alive, you just have to look for it— and if you don't see any, then start spreading some yourself!

While you don't necessarily have to start using "Yes, ma'am" and "No, sir" on a consistent basis, a couple of easy, gracious phrases to implement are "Please" and "Thank you." It sounds like a kindergarten rule, but surprisingly few people use these simple, rudimentary manners anymore. Politeness can start by simply reinstating a "Please" the next time you ask a coworker to hand you the stapler. You could offer a sincere "Thank you" to the waiter who brings your food. Try being a gracious driver and letting the car ahead of you into the traffic-jam line. Compliment the grocery-store cashier on her manicured nails. Offer an elderly person or a pregnant lady your seat in the waiting area. These are such rare occurrences and expressions these days that it just might make that person's day.

Another thing I advocate: using polite speech without losing who you are. For example, in the South, phrases like "We're fixin' to leave" and "I got a hankerin' for catfish" are pretty common; they may not be textbook grammar, but they are so endearing and charming I don't ever want them to die. Many of my friends have made it their goal to ditch the accent entirely, but that kind of makes me want to cry; you certainly don't need to go that far and completely lose that congenial charm. Wherever you're from, stay true to yourself!

My husband is from Minnesota (or as they say, Minnes-o-o-o-ta), and now, after having spent lots of time there (I pretty much make him drive alternating routes between the Mall of America and the nearest Caribou Coffee), I've come to find just as much amusement in their extreme-Northern vernacular as I do in Southern speech: "Ya sure, you bet-cha," "O-o-h that mo-o-vie was super great," and "Yer gonna hafta see this!" Again, I never want them to lose their Minnes-o-o-ta-ness. I'm from the Midwest, so I probably fall under that nonregional dialect category, along with everybody else from an "I" state: Iowa, Indiana, Illinois... What about you? What does your accent (or the lack thereof) reveal about you and where you're from?

People always say that Spanish, Portuguese, French, Italian, and Romanian are the Romance languages. What does that make English? The cheap date language? (I was an English major, so I'm allowed to make these kinds of cracks, right?)

Nevertheless, when was the last time you heard someone talk and thought it was really beautiful? Julie Andrews has a lovely way of speaking, and she notably doesn't use "like" or "umm" every fifth word. Morgan Freeman has a calm, steady delivery and is always very deliberate in his enunciations.

How do we avoid language pitfalls and cultivate a vocabulary that sounds polished? We'll delve into more details later, but we can start by putting down our phones, picking up a book, and staying informed. I'm also going to try deleting a few "I dunnos" and inserting a couple more "I would be honored tos" into my daily rhetoric, just for good measure.

We live in a day and age saturated with the marvels of technology—from Internet cat videos and game apps to streaming services and Netflix binges—we spend a lot of time in front of those little screens. Unfortunately, that can be addicting and counterproductive. Especially when you're supposed to be studying for a big exam or listening intently to a friend's boyfriend woes. Don't get me wrong, I could easily watch nothing but reruns of *Gilmore Girls* for the rest of my life and be perfectly happy. But sadly, having the ability to list Rory's boyfriends in chronological order won't get me very far in life.

My sister and I grew up with only four channels on our TV and thought we were really roughing it, since our entertainment options were usually limited to the local PBS telethon or *TGIF*. We pined for luxuries like the Disney Channel and Nickelodeon, and we listened with sheer incredulity to tales of a magical airwave called the Cartoon Network. When our friends would invite us over to spend the night, we'd hungrily consume hours of *Clarissa Explains It All* and *Are You Afraid of the Dark?* Recently, though, I was talking about childhood stories with a band I used to work with. The group consists of four brothers in their twenties, and they actually grew up with *no* TV. Not just "we-only-had-one-in-the-family-room" or "all-we-had-was-a-small-set-in-the-kitchen." *Nothing.*

Now, these four guys are some of the most hardworking, competent, and talented young people I've met in a long time. I asked them the reason for their familial musical ability, and the lead singer said to me, "Well, actually we're just really thankful that our parents didn't have a TV. Instead of plopping down in front of the television after school, we were forced to get creative—play instruments, practice, learn techniques from other musicians. We would never be where we are today if we would have had a television to watch." That certainly gave me a new perspective on my own upbringing (I don't exactly have a record deal to show for my cableless childhood, though, just a bunch of papier-mâché books about my two cats, Justin and Fluffy).

If you haven't quite reached that extreme screen-shunning stage, I completely understand. I'm not at the point where I've eliminated all entertainment either. But it's easier than you might think to set small, offscreen goals for yourself. If you find yourself in front of a screen for four-plus hours a day, try paring down your time to just an hour each day. If you watch two or three shows a week, try just one. You'll be amazed at how many other things you have time for. But what do you do with all that free time? The possibilities are endless, but it can be tricky getting started.

When I first tried cutting out TV, I remember plunking down on the couch and staring vacantly at the blank screen, waiting for instructions as to what I should do next. It took me several weeks to get into a groove of doing *other* things first, rather than zapping on the tube pronto when I walked in the door. The easiest thing I found, and my first recommendation, is to *read a book*.

Beyond the obvious benefits (improved vocabulary, widened worldview, etc.), studies have shown that reading can physically reduce your stress. According to a study conducted at the University of Sussex, just six minutes of reading a day can reduce your stress levels by 68 percent.[10] That's crazy! Additionally, reading beat out various other forms of relaxation including playing video games, walking, listening to music, and drinking coffee or tea. That's pretty powerful stuff.

But let's be honest: For some people, reading can be a daunting task. My mother was a reading teacher for thirty-three years, and before I could walk, I would crawl to our book drawer to read, so I'm probably a little biased. But I do know the most common question from my nonreader friends is, Where do I start? The huge sea of material to choose from can be overwhelming. To help you cultivate your inner bookworm, take the following quiz to find out which kind of book is best for you. Simply choose whichever answer sounds most like you.

## What Kind of Bookworm Are You?

1. If I have a free Saturday all to myself, I will usually:
   a. Ride my bike to the park or call up a few friends to go hiking.
   b. Pull on my new swimsuit and head for the nearest pool, beach, or open patch of grass.
   c. Take a tour of the current art exhibit on display at the museum.
2. When I'm surfing the Internet, I typically spend most of my time:
   a. Looking up airfare prices for my next spontaneous getaway.
   b. Updating Twitter and shopping online at Revolve.
   c. Reading up on the day's headline news while e-mailing.
3. When my roommate/significant other is gone for the weekend, my guilty-pleasure movie of choice is:

    a. *Million Dollar Baby.*

    b. *Legally Blonde.*

    c. *Gone with the Wind.*

4. If I could have dinner with anyone in the world, I would most likely pick:

    a. Kerri Walsh Jennings.

    b. Chris Hemsworth.

    c. A US president.

5. When I set foot in the mall, I make a beeline for:

    a. Foot Locker—my running shoes are currently being held together with duct tape.

    b. J.Crew—can you say, madras plaid?!

    c. Best Buy—the new Raconteurs album is out, and I can't read the liner notes on iTunes.

6. If I won a free vacation anywhere in the world, I would:

    a. Take a safari in Africa—sleep under the stars, see wild animals, hike Kilimanjaro.

    b. Relax in the Land Down Under—soak up the sun, go snorkeling off the Great Barrier Reef, visit the Sydney Opera House.

    c. Take an old-world tour of Europe—see the architecture, learn history, eat cheese.

7. When I think of my dream house, I envision a:

    a. Rustic mountain home somewhere in the mountains.

    b. Beachy cottage close to the water.

    c. Historic mansion that's been restored.

**If you picked mostly A's:** Go get a suspense/thriller/mystery novel! You have a heart for adventure and are constantly on the go. You like being spontaneous and are quick, smart, driven, and perceptive. You love movies like *Ocean's Thirteen* and *Edge of Tomorrow.* A good mystery or suspense story with a well-developed plot will hold your attention, and you might enjoy authors such as G. K. Chesterton, John Grisham, Frank Peretti, or Janet Evanovich.

**If you picked mostly B's:** You are a prime chick-lit candidate! You are easygoing yet passionate and probably enjoy shopping, going for walks, and reading magazines by the pool. You love to have fun and you enjoy movies like *Bridget Jones's Baby* and *Sleepless in Seattle.* Lighthearted, humorous, and character-driven stories will keep you reading, and you'll really appreciate authors such as Jane Austen, Sophie Kinsella, Anne Lamott, or Lauren Weisberger.

**If you picked mostly C's:** We've got a historical-fiction reader on our hands! You are a romantic and love reading about history, culture, and issues. You love to escape to different worlds and days of old yet appreciate a good sense of humor. You love movies like *Elizabeth* and *Sense and Sensibility.* Intelligent, well-written, and captivating historical fiction will keep you entertained for hours, and you may like authors such as Francine Rivers, Philippa Gregory, Michelle Moran, or Robert Hicks. If you're in need of a little extra guidance, look no further.

---

### 5 More Ways to Discover the Right Book for You

1. Don't overdo it. No one says you have to run out and tackle *The History of the Decline and Fall of the Roman Empire*. Start off with something short, like a collection of short stories or essays, or a novella.
2. Get into YA selections. Young adult novels aren't just for teens, and they can be real page-turners. Tons of YA books have also been made into blockbuster movies, including *The Maze Runner* and *The Giver*, so try reading the book before seeing the movie and then decide which is better.
3. Ask for help. Take a trip to your local library or independent bookstore. Tell the librarian or bookstore employee a little about what interests you—many times they have great suggestions or can at least steer you in the right direction.
4. Go online. Join a social media site for booklovers, like Goodreads, and peruse what your friends are reading and loving for ideas.
5. Try audiobooks. You can listen while driving or working out at the gym—they are available for free from your local library. Simply download them right to your smartphone.

---

If you're still not feeling the book thing, another great way to up the language ante is to learn a new one. Audrey Hepburn knew several languages, including Dutch, English, French, Italian, and Spanish. Obviously, she was more than just a pretty face! You'll also learn more about the world and other cultures. Learning a new language is not for the faint of heart, though. I've spent a collective four years studying

Spanish and still feel pretty limited in my abilities—it's not for lack of my teachers trying, though. I think I'm just not gifted when it comes to learning new languages. Perhaps that's why I went running for the English department when it came time to pick a major.

If you're not quite up for a complete language makeover, it can also be fun and enlightening to simply immerse yourself in a new culture. There's no teacher like experience, right? Start by studying up on your favorite country—learn the history, customs, holidays, and traditions of the country. You'll learn so much about their language just by studying the names of towns, cities, and families. Then start saving for a trip to spend a few days there. Convince a friend or two to come along with you and make it a spring break getaway or even an annual tradition. Just do your homework on a safe place to stay.

One of my best friends, Blair, spent nine months in Kyrgyzstan and upon returning to the United States enrolled in all kinds of Russian literature and language classes. She fell in love with their culture and wanted to experience as much of it as she could. Another good friend, Ruthanne, lived in China for a year, taught English in an elementary school, and still loves to talk about the culture, people, and languages years later. Somehow, when it's a place or subject that is truly personal and fascinating to us, it's not work learning it. Even if you don't have the time or resources to take a year off and explore a foreign country, you can check out lonelyplanet.com, read some travel memoirs, or subscribe to a monthly travel magazine.

Not thrilled with the idea of traveling overseas? No problem! There is plenty to see right here in the good ol' US of A. My editor loves to research a city, scope out the local art galleries, museums, and historical tours, and then book a weekend getaway for herself. If it's within driving distance, she makes it a road trip. She spends the days exploring the city and taking pictures, then, at night, she finds great new restaurants and food to try. Back in my prebaby days, I loved traveling by myself to a new city, visiting all the bookish sites (public libraries, off-the-beaten-path bookstores), and making a pit stop at the nearest Ivy League school (I *told* you I'm a nerd). No matter where you choose to go—be it London or your living room—have fun exploring and expanding your knowledge.

Journaling is another effortless outlet to improve your speech and develop your interests. Overall, people tend to filter out the "likes" and "umm maybes" when they're jotting down their thoughts and feelings in a diary. Your natural self will come out more readily when you're alone with your thoughts and not influenced by outside speech, friends' conversations, music, or movies. I began keeping a daily journal in fifth grade, and it's one of the best things I've ever done. Not only is it superbly entertaining to go back and read about the things that were soooooo important to me at the time (I *for sure* wasn't going to marry Darin C. after he smashed a s'more in my hair during that field trip to the science museum), but you can take stock of how much you've grown and matured, even over the course of one year.

The journaling process is often extremely therapeutic. Doug Addison, a writer and expert on dream interpretation, recommends journaling once a day. "It is not about quantity, it's getting yourself in the habit of doing it that counts," Doug says. "Find the best time for yourself to journal. For me it's early in the morning, but maybe you're an afternoon or night person. The important thing is: capture those dreams and make notes."[11]

A journal is a safe place to take out all our aggressions; my notebook has yet to complain about all the abuse I've heaped on it over the years. Journaling also provides some much-needed alone time for us ladies on the go. Most of us probably don't even get a lunch break to ourselves, so just a few precious minutes alone in the morning or before we hit the hay can truly have a cathartic effect. Pick up a journal and keep it beside your bed. Or even jot things down in the Notes function on your phone—I use it constantly to take notes for books, writing projects, and the like. Even if it's not a daily occurrence, the act of simply taking time for yourself and sorting through your thoughts and emotions is healthy and helpful.

Besides documenting our hopes, dreams, and frustrated

venting about a boss, a journal provides a perfect space to create a Smart Girl list! We've explored several small steps toward becoming a more intelligent, well-spoken lady, but now it's time to put them into action. One of my old coworkers and I sat down and did this awhile back, and we've found it to be a great, concrete way to articulate our goals. Just as an example, I've included my own list of things I'd like to do to become a more articulate, knowledgeable, and well-rounded person:

### Jordan's Smart Girl List

1. Earn my master's degree.
2. Learn how to plant a garden (successfully).
3. Teach a college course on music and writing.
4. Learn a new word every day.
5. Take a trip to Greece.

Now it's your turn. What's something you're constantly thinking about accomplishing? Buying an LSAT study book and finally signing yourself up for the test? Volunteering to mentor a child after school? Reading at least one book a month? Taking a French class and rewarding yourself with that trip to Paris? Signing up for a cooking course at your local culinary arts school? Take some time to really think about your options and aspirations, and then grab a piece of paper and ink out all your well-spoken, well-informed Smart Girl goals. Then go do them!

## My Smart Girl List

1. _____

2. _____

3. _____

4. _____

5. _____

Words have power, as do our thoughts and goals before we've even officially formulated them. That's why it's crucial to record them—you never know when you might have the solution to a global problem. You may invent a new technology that streamlines social media. You might sketch a brand-new design trend. You might discover the cure for cancer. Never discount yourself and what you're capable of.

After all of the reading, journaling, and self-informing you're doing, you will soon be bowling over colleagues, friends, and family members with your eloquent rhetoric and erudite self. Don't be discouraged by a momentary flub or blooper—you were destined to be a history maker with your words! People will take notice of your enlightened discourse and will inevitably be attracted to, and want to join in, the pursuit of your highly developed language.

*Chapter Five*

# Use Some Elbow Grease

"Nobody ever drowned in his own sweat." —*Ann Landers*

I come from a long line of hard workers and überproductive people. It's basically my legacy to love to work. In fact, I begged my mom to drive me to my first job when I was fourteen—eventually I got my license and was able to chauffeur myself around, but the fact remains, I've always loved work. For some reason, I get a sick amount of satisfaction out of it. It's kind of a problem, actually. Nevertheless, the possession of a good work ethic is not just helpful in terms of navigating the job market—it can positively, or negatively, affect every aspect of your life (more on that later).

It's easy to become disillusioned about hard work, good ethics, and real accomplishments, but there are actually so many modern stories of success. The political landscape alone is worth noting—there has been an amazing influx of female candidates lately. The business world is no different—women are moving and shaking their way to the top. Here are just a few examples of inspiring, successful women:

**Mina Guli**—Athlete, adventurer, and CEO of Thirst. Mina recently ran across seven deserts on seven continents in just seven weeks to raise awareness about water scarcity.

**Jenny Fleiss and Jenn Hyman**—Cofounders of Rent the Runway. Jenny and Jenn launched their business as a way of providing designer dress and accessory rentals to anyone at a discounted rate.

**Susan Wojcicki**—CEO of YouTube. In addition to coming up with countless innovative ideas and strategies for Google and YouTube, she's also a mom to five kids and an advocate for family-work balance.

**Jennifer Lee**—Screenwriter and film director. Not only was she the first female director of a Walt Disney Animation Studios feature film, but she went on to become the first female director of a feature film that earned more than $1 billion in gross box-office revenue.[12]

**Zhou Qunfei**—Entrepreneur and founder of touch-screen maker Lens Technology. She started out as a factory worker and has gone on to become the world's richest self-made woman.

**Nikki Haley**—First female governor of South Carolina. She started out working as a bookkeeper for her parents' clothing store at age thirteen and has gone on to become the second Indian American governor in the United States.[13]

Our society still rewards a strong work ethic, and that's what it takes to make it. No matter what industry you're trying to break into—interior design, medical school, counseling, sports—the same rules still apply. The one who puts in the most time and effort is going to get the spot. And lest you think your job is eternally secure, you've got to maintain that hustle to make sure someone smarter, faster, and more talented doesn't come along and snatch it away from you. Nothing is guaranteed in life. Nothing is certain. You've got to work to earn it.

No matter what it seems like, it's not all about *who* you know, it's *what* you know. Sure, friends or colleagues can help to make an initial connection, but after that, you're on your own. You've got to prove yourself and show that you've got what it takes. A letter of recommendation can only get you so far. A cousin's call on your behalf to an employer can only get your foot in the door. Beyond that, it's up to you. Are *you* going to work to make that deadline? Are *you* going to come in early to get things ready for the day? Be ready to serve and do menial tasks. You will never be too big to get your hands dirty. Never. If you want to continue to progress in your career, then just plan on putting in long hours, late nights, and early mornings. And when you're exhausted and think you won't make it another day, go get some coffee and get back at it. When the going gets tough, the tough get going to ... somewhere with caffeine!

How do we begin? Where do we start? If we're shooting for the stars, aren't we supposed to simply wait for our rocket to come pick us up? Sometimes others' jobs and positions can look like the lazy river at a water park—it seems like they just drifted into that position and are layin' back, takin' it easy. You wonder, *Why wasn't it that easy for me? Can't I have it all, too?* But the thing about a lazy river is that you don't see all the prep work it took to get there. There was the purchasing of a swimsuit, the applying of sunscreen, the packing of the beach bag, the driving to the water park, the long line to get into said park, the reading of the map to find the lazy river, the tube rental to get *into* the lazy river—you get my point. It's easy to look at someone who's "arrived" and think they've got it made. But the truth is, everyone's had to start somewhere. Sure, some people have an easier time than others, but everyone has had to put in some measure of work. It doesn't just happen. You've got to work to get there!

Life can appear ominous when you're barely perched on the first rung of the corporate ladder. It can seem that your goals are far, far away. Surely there must be a shortcut? An instant dream-producing pill to take? Many times, shortcuts end up being more like lo-o-o-ngcuts. The best way to do things is usually the old-fashioned way. Take time to do your homework, build something slowly, and pour your heart and soul into it. If it's meant to be, you'll eventually reach your goals. If something seems too easy, too quick, and too good to be true, it probably is. You don't need to craft yourself a tinfoil hat and be skeptical of every opportunity that comes along; simply strive to use wisdom and discretion when making decisions. And most importantly, don't give up! Your finish line may be closer than you think. In fact, having a far-flung dream can make you more determined than ever to prove that hard work really does pay off in the long run. And there's usually only one place to start. You guessed it—at the bottom.

Sometimes the bottom doesn't look so good, though. The bottom is kinda dark, dirty, and stinky. If you don't believe me, go listen to AC/DC's song "It's a Long Way to the Top (If You Wanna Rock 'n' Roll)." It takes humility, character, and commitment to work your way up. It takes a positive attitude and a can-do spirit. Don't bother showing up if you're not willing to put in the effort. There are other people waiting to take your spot, so save the company the time-consuming interview process.

I was always somewhat insecure about my background. I was from the middle of nowhere. I didn't have any names to drop. It seemed there were about a majillion other people trying to make it in Music City; what did I have to offer? However, rather than seeing your past as a liability, let it be what sets you apart. There's only one you, and the *real* you is what the world needs. Not some flawless, made-up version of yourself that looks and sounds a lot like everyone else. The you that's from a town no one's ever heard of, the you with no famous parents. *That's* the you the world needs.

My friend and former publicist for Warner Music Group, Amanda Collins, attributes her success in a male-dominated business to having been surrounded by strong, confident, intelligent women her entire life. "Beginning with my mom, who rose to be the COO of the company at which she worked, and throughout my career, I have been encouraged by successful women who taught me that hard work and believing that I have the ability to effect change will allow me to realize my goals." Now the vice president of corporate communications for NBC Universal, she also says, "Business is business. What should matter is a person's ability to take business to the next level. When I walk into a meeting, I want people to see me for what I can contribute to the success of the company. I hold myself to that same standard and see my colleagues based not on their gender or background, but rather on their decisions, actions, and contributions to the team."

How do we get from point A to *that*? You can think of your career as one giant résumé—it will have definite starting and stopping points and will follow a natural progression. If it's a good résumé, it will inevitably evolve and change—but should always show growth and personal development, just like your career. To get started, you'll want to make sure your cover letter is in shipshape condition.

## Cover Letter 101

📄 **Keep it handy.** A cover letter is a pretty standard document that you'll want to edit and maintain throughout your career and job-searching process. Save it to your desktop (if you're kickin' it old-school), or keep it as a PDF file on your phone for quick access.

📄 **Keep it current.** Be sure to correctly distinguish between the current person you're addressing and the other dozen cover letters you sent out last week. The manager of social media marketing over at Corporate Giant No. 1 doesn't want to accidentally read the letter you wrote to the director of design at the boutique firm down the street. Double- and triple-check names and facts, just to be sure.

📄 **Keep it short.** This is not the spot to show off your auto-biographical skills. While you may have a fascinating life story, keep personal facts and anecdotes to a minimum. Limit it to a few lines about your work history and how your personal goals align with the company's mission statement.

📄 **Keep it light.** This is just a brief introduction between yourself and the company; think of it as a blind date—they may not want to hear all your deep, dark secrets on the first night. Keep it positive and casual, while still being professional.

📄 **Keep it neat.** There is a distinct order and flow of organization within a cover letter. I would encourage you to do some quick online searches for a template. As tempting as it may be to stray from the norm, most employers will view this as an indicator of your inability to follow directions. When in doubt, stick to the template!

When you're in the cover letter stage, it can be incredibly helpful to do a little networking. Do you want to work at a magazine? Find out when the publisher's next social gathering is and make yourself available to chat with anyone and everyone there. Do you want to break into the music industry? Hit up a local songwriters' night in your area and make pals with fellow musicians and prospective label execs. Are you hoping to get that political-campaign gig? Join your candidate of choice's street team and start making an impact in your immediate community. Wherever your interest lies, don't be afraid to start small.

Another really great resource that isn't tapped into much anymore is mentoring. A mentor can be anyone—from an older colleague, to a pastor, to a relative—just someone you trust to give wise counsel and guidance. Mentors can be a *huge* source of knowledge and inspiration in the career-finding, soul-searching period of complete befuddlement in our lives. So if you happen to find wise, caring, and trustworthy sources within your prospective industry, you should definitely draw on them for helpful hints, contacts, and all-around encouragement! You might be surprised to find that most people are more than willing to give recommendations, introduce you to prospective employers, and just generally be of service. It was a sweet, unassuming adjunct professor in college who not only encouraged me in my writing, but helped me land my first job in the music industry; I am still so grateful for him to this day.

Regardless of your final goal—be it corporate publicity or local coffee shop entrepreneur, there is a universal message that can be applied to every situation: There is no substitute for simply *trying*. Which brings us to the résumé stage of this process. Ultimately, we can sit around and talk about all that we're going to accomplish, but unless we actually get out and do it, nothing will happen. So when all else fails, put in an application! Here are some hints to keep around when composing and polishing your résumé.

### Résumé 101

✓ **Be the posting.** Don't be afraid to go over an employer's job posting with a fine-tooth comb. Get a feel for what they're really looking for (i.e., are they looking for a team player or a self-motivated individual?). Do they require five-plus years of experience, or a semester-long internship? The company should be able to tell you the exact qualities they're looking for so you can determine if you match their criteria. Then tailor your résumé to each individual posting—while it's awesome that you won that classical music award, a better position to note on your application for math teacher might be your semester-long gig at a geometry learning center. Highlight your specific interests, accomplishments, and experience based on what job you're applying for.

✓ **Be open.** If it's a position that requires a definitive degree (doctor, lawyer, teacher, etc.), make sure you fit the basic requirements. Other careers are more lenient with their qualifications and might even offer to train you in certain areas.

✓ **Be simple.** While it may be tempting to make your résumé stand out with fancy fonts and formatting, it's the information that you want to shine. If arranging your résumé in an artistic way makes it hard for someone to read it quickly, you're hurting rather than helping yourself. Worse, some formatting can conflict with a company's system, cutting off parts of the text or even making it not show up at all.

✓ **Be sure.** Check, recheck, and check again all the tedious facts and info on your résumé (e.g., the phone numbers for your references, the URL for your old Internet start-up). On one occasion, I was helping a college student prepare a résumé and cover letter for a job in the music industry and discovered a very inappropriate-sounding typo in her mission statement. The catastrophe was avoided, but the fact remains: It never hurts to check!

✓ **Be able to fill in the gaps.** Gaping holes, such as unexplained yearlong breaks, stick out on a résumé. Even if you did deliberately take a year off to go backpacking through Europe, find some way to spin that downtime as being beneficial to your career. Did you learn some of the language, take classes, or gain an understanding of the culture? Were you involved in nonprofit work that helped you hone your personal mission statement? Find some way to turn that time into a good thing professionally as well as personally.

✓ **Be optimistic.** Don't get discouraged if you don't get a call back. Act as though each application is your first (even if it's your seventy-fourth). One of them will be the right one. Remember, if you possess the right skill set, they'll be just as excited to snag you for their team as you are to be on their team.

For many, the next inevitable stage of work is an internship. Many companies and corporations offer college credit for internships these days, making it a win-win situation. You get college credit, awesome real-world experience, and the chance to find out if the company is hiring (providing you enjoyed your stay there...If you had a horrible internship, it's still a win because you've come to the important realization that you never want to work there!). In addition, the employer gets some free help, as well as the chance to see if you're employee material. It's a great system, and I would encourage anyone and everyone to get involved. Check to see if your local university and/or place of desired employment participates in an intern program. Even if a company doesn't offer college credit, it certainly doesn't hurt to inquire about a paid internship or even a part-time volunteer position. It's a great way to get your foot in the door.

Some may sniff at an unpaid position or a college-credit-only gig, but just remember, it's an opportunity and privilege that many other young people around the world would die for. So rather than having the attitude of *What can this company do for me?* turn it around and ask, *What can I do for this company?* Think, *How can I make them look great? How can I be of service? How can I be an asset?* Don't expect anyone to roll out the red carpet for you or hold your hand while you complete a simple task. Instead, look for ways to improve, streamline, or enrich day-to-day operations, and soon you'll be moving on to a bigger and better position.

That old saying "A little dirt never hurt" extends beyond the days of getting sand in our mouths on the playground. If you really want to succeed and pursue your passion, there's going to be a lot of long hours, sacrifices, and, yes, possibly crying (I cried at work only once—the day I put in my two weeks' notice—Kelly Cutrone would be so proud). You might have to cancel a few dates with the boyfriend, neglect a concert or two with the gang, and probably eat a few meals out of the vending machine. It won't be pretty for a while, my friends, but you'll get through it.

Likewise, there are equally many ways to go about making a good impression at work and keeping your position. First of all, be willing to go above and beyond the call of duty. Employers are looking to see what you will do with the task that's been assigned to you—have you done exactly what you've been asked to do, or have you gone out of your way to do *more* than was required? There's always someone who will do *just* enough. And that someone is the one who didn't get the job. Have you been going the distance and yet it appears that you're being overlooked? You may think that your efforts are going unnoticed, but I'm telling you this as one who's been there—an employer can *easily* spot the one who's excited about their work and eager to tackle the next project. Those who do more than others expect or need always stand head and shoulders above the ones who do just enough to scrape by. Lauren Conrad got her start interning in the *Teen Vogue* offices and she's now a certified fashion powerhouse. You never know where a little elbow grease might take you.

The point is, don't be afraid to get your hands dirty with menial tasks during this stage of your career. One of my old bosses, Derek, was the best at this. Even though he was the vice president of our department, he would join in on the tedious chore of stuffing, addressing, and mailing out hundreds of CDs by hand every month. His encouraging, down-to-earth attitude was contagious and made the whole process a fun experience. Think you're better than janitorial jobs and mailroom duties? Smile and sing "Hi-ho, hi-ho, it's off to work I go!" while you're doing it. Feel like you're above ripping out carpet staples and hauling massive ceramic urns down a busy street (that was the day I realized a career in interior design was more than just picking out paint colors)? Keep a happy face and ask, "What's next?" even when you're ready to collapse. You may very well be above licking those invitation envelopes for your boss's Christmas party, but make them the best-licked invitations your boss has ever seen and soon you'll be moving on to bigger and better things. Need a few more pointers and tips for your first internship? Look no further.

### Interning 101

**Master the basics.** Things like punctuality and professionalism might seem like rudimentary elements, but in an intern setting, everything is magnified. This is your chance to show the entire company who you are and what you're made of, and even a few mornings of coming in late are basically the equivalent of stamping a big, red NOPE on your forehead. You might think, *Oh, I just overslept again, no biggie*... But the employer sees that and thinks, *If she can't handle a simple task like getting to work on time, how could I trust her with a major account?*

**Spread the love.** Get out of your comfort zone and meet other employees during your time there. Explore other departments and find out what their day looks like. If you're not feeling your specific position, that doesn't mean the perfect job doesn't exist just down the hall. Make a point to become familiar with different people, and positions, within the company. This can only help you when it comes time to apply for a real job.

**Go for the gold.** Just as Olympic athletes didn't get to where they are by simply putting in the base-level required training, getting a great job is about working harder and faster than the average busy bee. I know we've already touched on this, but it's worth repeating: Go above and beyond what's asked of you if you want to advance. If you find that you have extra time on your hands, look for something that needs to be done that you can handle and offer to take care of it. Even something as simple as organizing the chaotic supply cabinet can make a positive impression.

**Do the time.** Most internships have definite start and end dates, so make the most of every minute there. Ask your supervisor to go to lunch one day (your treat) so you can pick her or his brain about business. Make plans to attend your company's annual picnic and do some networking. Get to know as much as you can, while you can. Even if you ultimately decide that the place or occupation isn't for you, see the merit in the experience and weigh the value of being able to check another option off your career list.

Blame it on the day job, but I've heard lots of great stories about how people got that first foot in the door in the music industry. My friend Jill was a waitress at a nice restaurant that one of the record label's executives liked to frequent. She ended up waiting on him several times, and he was so impressed with her service and attention to detail that he recommended her for a job the next time an opening came up. Another one of my friends, Anna, started out helping friends and musicians select outfits for their upcoming music videos, concerts, and other appearances. She became so popular that she eventually launched her own clothing line and now styles artists and actors for movies and red-carpet events. I used to sit next to another now-famous country singer during a creative writing class in college. He worked full-time to support himself and took night classes as well while pursuing a career in music. Soon he was playing sold-out arenas and major award shows. You never know what opportunities might arise when you are faithfully serving at your current position to the best of your ability. It gives new meaning to the old saying "Bloom where you are planted."

I have no doubt there are dozens of other stories similar to these from all different industries. The music industry is one of those bizarro worlds that sometimes doesn't require a "standard" interview; however, the basic principles still apply (unless you're Lady Gaga, then there really are no rules). The bottom line is that it takes persistence and dedication to get to where we want to go. Perhaps you've already laid that groundwork, and, after relentless networking, sending out dozens of résumés, and cold-calling everyone and their dog, you finally hear back from a prospective employer—you've got an interview. What a ridiculously frightening process. For some pointers on how to prep for the interview, read on.

## Interviewing 101

🐾 **Practice, practice, practice.** Start by reciting your answers in the bathroom mirror, then get someone else to help you with a mock interview. Make it as realistic as possible—you can even meet them for lunch or coffee to simulate the real deal. Make them throw you some curveballs just for the heck of it. You never know what the employer might ask, so it's best to be prepared.

🐾 **Plan, plan, plan.** Interviews can take a variety of different forms, so be sure that you know in advance what the situation will be. They might be conducted in a group setting, over Skype, on the phone, in person—you name it. Make sure that you're familiar with the format. Do you know the basics of joining a conference call? Are you prepared to be interviewed by a panel? Will the interview be online or in some sort of video format? If so, make sure your computer is compatible and do a few test runs with a friend to confirm that your mic is working and the screen is centered. Then be sure you're seated in a place with decent lighting. You worked hard to pick out that perfect interview jacket—you want them to be able to see it! Double-check the background for any distracting pictures or decor—remember: *You* want to be the focal point.

🐾 **Location, location, location.** Find out the location of the interview beforehand if possible. If it's going to take place at a restaurant downtown, do a little recon and scope out good parking so you don't end up driving around the block forty times and missing your interview. If it's at an office, drive there at least a day before so you know you can find it. Will they be calling you at home? Make sure you're in a location with noise control. The last thing you want is for the F train to go whizzing by while you're in the middle of making your big speech about your work ethic and have them miss the whole thing.

And, finally, take a deep breath. No matter what happens, you'll be okay. People have nailed, and blown, interviews many times throughout history. You won't be the first to do either! When in doubt, consult this Top Ten List to help you feel confident and prepared. Don't worry, you've got this.

### Top Ten Ways to Get Hired

10. Plan on being at least fifteen minutes early. Something might go awry, and you'll be thankful for the extra time; worst-case scenario, you'll just have to wait a few minutes.

9. Dress appropriately—dress codes can differ by industry, but it never hurts to be conservative.

8. Read up on the company's history and become familiar with the job you're applying for.

7. Maintain eye contact—it shows confidence and assures them that you're paying attention.

6.  Have extra copies of your résumé on hand.

5.  Prepare two or three questions of your own to ask (just not about salary, yet)—it shows that you're genuinely interested and invested in the position.

4.  Practice a "What are your strengths and weaknesses?" answer. This is a pretty standard question, but it still trips up people.

3.  Be willing to share a little about your background and experience as well as talk up your willingness to learn a new skill or trade.

2.  Be honest: Did you get fired from your last job? Not complete high school? Commit a felony? Be upfront and truthful when you're asked about life details.

1.  Practice being well-spoken—no slang and no swearing. And spit out the gum. Nobody wants to see that big wad of Bubblicious.

Congratulations! You got the job. Now what? Whether you're knee-deep in the corporate rat race, simply starting out in the world of freelance work, or just trying to land that first restaurant gig, one of the most disruptive life changes when making the leap into the working world is arguably the schedule. When I first started my eight-to-five job, the 6 a.m. wake-up time was extremely disconcerting. The last time I had seen that time of day was in high school for that choir trip to New York when we all piled onto the bus in our bunny slippers at 3 a.m. The whole process can end up feeling a lot like *The Devil Wears Prada*; just when you drift off from the night before, you hear the loathsome alarm and groggily reach for the snooze button...morning after morning, consistently seeing times of day that you never thought humanly possible and being so tired that you honestly can no longer tell if you're asleep, awake, or just dreaming about being asleep. The relentless routine of rising early and not-getting-home-until-dark-thirty is a huge adjustment, not to mention the fact that your life is pretty much over for five out of seven days of the week. It takes specific rearranging of priorities, commitments, and grocery shopping.

Aside from the weekends, those after-hours shenanigans are probably going to dwindle (I'm kind of an eighty-five-year-old grandma at heart, so late nights weren't too difficult for me to give up). And since sleeping in is no longer an option, it takes only about a week of 2 a.m. Waffle House runs and 6 a.m. wake-up calls before you'll throw in the towel and succumb to the 10 p.m. corporate-world bedtime. But after you get the hang of it, mornings aren't so bad. The sun is shining, the birds are singing...All right, I'll be honest, I'm one of those obnoxious morning people who come into work singing "Zip-A-Dee-Doo-Dah" and talking about how great it is to be alive. But the late-night sacrifices really are completely worth it to know at the end of the day that you've put in a productive day at work.

If you have no aspirations or couldn't care less about getting a promotion, then, by all means, continue doing the bare minimum. But the best way to show you're interested in sticking around is to do just that: Stick around. Offer to stay late to help with menial tasks, or volunteer to oversee a tedious report that the senior partners hate. They'll be grateful for the help and eager to get to know the good Samaritan who chipped in. If you're getting your work done efficiently, look for opportunities to take on new challenges; and if you don't see any opportunities, ask for them. Showing that you're capable and able to do more complicated work is how you can establish that you're ready for a promotion. Just make sure that you're also keeping on top of the work you were hired to do, or it might backfire and make you look like you can't handle your job.

When you're in the throes of the daily grind, it's also crucial to keep a sane perspective on things. While I tend to hate the phrase "It's not personal, it's just business," it does have its merit. I certainly don't advocate being cold and calculating, but it's good to remember that not everything is a personal attack against you. Work is just work, and people are probably going to say things that will hurt your feelings. You may get left out or passed up for a promotion. I know it can be momentarily discouraging, but it's not the end of your story. There are politics and hierarchies at almost every job, so don't be surprised if you find yourself in the middle of office drama.

Continue to keep a good attitude and the situation will more than likely blow over. Just remember: There's more to you than this job.

My mom is great at advice in general but has given me some particularly significant hints in this department. I've had a lot of jobs: corn detassler, restaurant pianist, bookstore cashier, lifeguard, sales associate, online editor, concert tour coordinator, the list goes on and on—and I have thoroughly enjoyed most of them. But suddenly, when I quit my job at the record label to become an official SAHM (stay-at-home-mom), I took (and still sometimes take) everything horrifically personally. If my baby wouldn't eat green beans, I was a failure. If I didn't get the cat's litter box changed, I was a failure. Then I got sick and wasn't physically able to write, which, of course, made me a complete and *utter* failure. I had to learn to view it the same way that I'd viewed every other job—it wasn't personal, it was just business. At the office, if I had a particularly crazy day, I wouldn't beat myself up; I'd simply log off my computer and think of all the things that went right that day and mentally pat myself on the back for the few little victories I *did* have. If necessary, I'd come in early the next day to catch up and that would be that. It was no different with this new mom job. I had to retrain myself not to take it personally, any of it. Granted, my new career involved dirty diapers and sticky juice spills—as opposed to bands with bios and press releases that needed to be finalized. But it was kind of the same.

If it helps, let yourself off the hook emotionally. Sometimes it's easier to compartmentalize areas of our lives rather than letting them all go straight to our hearts. It's easier for me. I'm sure the psychology behind this theory is incredibly disturbing. Nevertheless, I'm thankful for the lesson learned and for my ever-patient teacher (I love you, Mom).

Last, but certainly not least, keep a positive attitude. No one enjoys working with someone who constantly whines and complains, so unless you're being asked to clean your employer's dog poo out of the carpet (heck, even if you are), try to keep a pleasant attitude. Not only will it motivate you to carry on, it's contagious. A smile and an optimistic outlook go a long, long way—you have no idea how much someone else at work might need to hear an encouraging word or just see a cheerful face. Rather than spreading gossip and ill will, try to be friendly and a good listener—chances are your coworker is as stressed as you are. If you're in need of some more on-the-job guidance, look no further. Here are a few ways to transition to the working world and maintain positivity at your new job.

### On the Job 101

📓 **Make friends with your alarm.** Save your Netflix marathons for the weekend and head to bed at a decent time. I know it's almost physically painful to force yourself to bed at an hour like 9 p.m., but your body and mind will thank you the next day.

🗂 **Make the most of the watercooler.** Notorious for being the home of the rumor mill, the office watercooler or kitchen can also be a place to make friends. Hang around for the latest chitchat about *The Bachelor* and see if anyone has any weekend plans, but don't linger too long—and politely excuse yourself if it starts to get gossipy.

🗂 **Make peace with your timeline.** While it can be tempting to post political commentary from your friends or retweet the latest news regarding your favorite band, try to put off personal social media time until you're done for the day. Most organizations do not relish the idea of your taking company time to post personal matters, so be respectful of their time and yours.

🗂 **Make nice with everyone.** You will be in close proximity with the people around you for many, many hours each week. So save the drama for your mama (actually, don't do that—your mama loves you) and put on your best face at work. Try to live in a peaceful existence with those around you. Don't let petty office issues or grievances ruin your rapport with your coworkers. Life is so much nicer when you enjoy the people you work with.

🗂 **Make sure to bring your water bottle.** This might seem like a silly thing, but you're going to be at work for many hours a day—potentially for the next twenty to thirty years.

It's best to get into a good hydration habit now. Most offices have a watercooler with cups, but it's a good idea to bring your own reusable water bottle. You'll most likely drink more water that way, and, additionally, you'll cut down on company waste.

**Be financially prepared.** When you get your first paycheck, you might be surprised by how much of it disappears before reaching your bank account to taxes, health care, and more taxes. Still, try to take advantage of any optional benefits the company offers. Electing to set aside pretax dollars for a 401(k), a health savings account, or transportation expenses from the start will be easier than having to adjust to less money later, and your future self will thank you. If you don't understand how these benefits work, ask someone in HR for help.

So you worked hard and finally landed your dream job. (Okay, maybe the six-by-six-foot cubicle isn't *really* your dream, but you're closer than you were before, right?) You're finally able to throw some of that grocery store sushi into the cart along with your ramen noodles, and your parents are temporarily satisfied that you have a steady job, "even though your mother and I paid all that money for you to go to school for art history and now you're just working at an online magazine." Things are looking up!

There's always room for advancement, though, right? What about a promotion? Or a move to a different company? How do you know when to go and when to stay? Is there an unspoken moral rule about what you should or shouldn't put up with in an office environment? Job transitions can be tricky business, so let's discuss.

Some work environments aren't for the timid—there can be negativity, backstabbing, rumors, and illegal activity. Nevertheless, that doesn't mean you need to take part in it. You just need to decide if it's worth it to stay. At the end of the day, only you can decide if some job, or job location, is worth sticking around for. I think that most of the time we intuitively know when something's not working. In the end, it's up to you and what you're comfortable with. Feel free to consult the following examples for help, but, ultimately, use your own discretion. Disclaimer: This is not legal advice, professional counseling, or a medical diagnosis—just the opinion of a girl who's had lots of jobs. Take it with a grain of salt.

## Transitions 101

**Scenario 1:** Your boss doesn't seem to notice the extra work you've been putting in and never compliments your efforts.

*Verdict:* STAY. Consider meeting with your boss to ask if there's something more you could be doing—you may be focusing on the wrong thing, but if you're on the right track, you can make your boss aware.

**Scenario 2**: A coworker tells you how you can get in on something that you believe is illegal, and she says you'll be the only one who's not involved if you say no.

*Verdict:* GO. That company is a ticking time bomb.

**Scenario 3:** You overhear some coworkers talking trash about a rival company and its employees.

*Verdict:* Refrain from engaging in their junior high antics and STAY.

**Scenario 4:** You've become the target of abusive e-mails and manipulative, controlling behavior.

*Verdict:* STAY *or* GO. You could report the behavior and wait it out, *or* start looking for another job—ultimately, you want to be somewhere you're respected and valued.

**Scenario 5:** Your boss always plays favorites, and some of your coworkers seem to spend more time undermining you than working.

*Verdict:* STAY *or* GO. Office politics exist everywhere, but depending on how bad the situation is, you may be happier with another group of people.

**Scenario 6:** A coworker keeps making subtle personal advances toward you that make you uncomfortable.

*Verdict:* Report the behavior to a supervisor or HR and STAY *or* GO (depending on what they decide to do with Mr. Creepy).

**Scenario 7:** You've been in your position much longer than your peers, but the promised promotion never comes through.

*Verdict:* GO. But secure a new job before turning in your two weeks' notice.


Sometimes it's difficult to know if you really *are* in a terrible situation or it's just life and you need to learn to deal with it. In either case, you can avoid personal injury by simply being yourself. No situation should warrant changing who you are to adapt to it. Even if everyone around you is involved in something shady, or if everyone is being treated terribly, don't feel as though you need to conform to your surroundings. Simply be your kind, intelligent self and either the situation will work itself out or you'll know it's time to move on. Personally, I always secretly wondered if I had what it took to make it in the business world because I wasn't very forward or confrontational. I still remember my sweet elementary school basketball coach telling me I needed to "be more aggressive," so I assumed that translated to the work world, too. Unfortunately, I couldn't handle an escalating argument or heated debate to save my life. My husband even tried to help; he would make me practice writing mean e-mails to him (then he would send it back and say, "Nope, this one has too many exclamation marks and smiley faces—try again"). All that to say, you can reach your goals by simply being you—naive smiley faces and all.

But what if nice goes unnoticed? If you've got a bazillion brilliant ideas that could revolutionize the place, don't be afraid to speak up. If you have a discerning and intelligent boss, it can never hurt to stop into his or her office, pitch a couple of ideas, and show that you're ready to take on more responsibilities. They'll see you as a team player and most likely start bringing you in for more meetings and brainstorming sessions. Let your creative juices flow!

But maybe you're stuck with a boss who doesn't give a rip about honesty, hard work, and starry-eyed small-town dreams. The higher-ups want movers and shakers and maybe even people who yell a lot. One of your greatest resources in this situation is the people around you. If you know you're a future editor in chief, start offering your editing and proof-reading services to fellow coworkers (people almost always welcome help when typing Christmas letters, writing out invitations, etc.). Word will quickly get around, and pretty soon you'll have enough recommendations from everyone in the office to approach someone higher up than your boss. Are you amazing with numbers? Make yourself a human calculator to the ones closest to you, and before you know it you'll have enough references to apply for that statistics position. Do you know that you take better pictures than everyone else put together in the print shop? Offer to shoot weddings, family portraits, and senior pictures for everyone you know, and soon you'll have a client base and a portfolio that speaks for itself. One of my friends' wives wanted to eventually open her own bakery, so she started making cakes for any and every occasion—including office baby showers and friends' birthday parties, and soon she had a great job at a bakery in town.

I love rags-to-riches stories. I think everyone does. This country was essentially built on such stories. My favorite writer, Louisa May Alcott, embodied the hard work and tenacity that are the main elements of the journey from rags to riches. Though her family was plagued by poverty, Louisa remained determined to make her mark on the world: "I *will* do something by and by. Don't care what, teach, sew, act, write, anything to help the family; and I'll be rich and famous and happy before I die, see if I won't!"[14] I wish she could have lived to see that her works have been made into movies and a Broadway musical, and that her books are being used as classic examples in schools and universities 150 years later. Of course, she went on to publish more than thirty books and short stories in her lifetime and finally achieved financial independence. But the thing she's most remembered for is her ability to capture the beauty of little domestic moments—getting up from a warm bed and going to work when it was freezing cold, failed attempts at trying a new recipe, making sure the pillows were fluffed for company—she's the absolute best at making mundane chores seem almost poetic (I'm borderline obsessed with Louisa, if you can't tell; my husband says he's drawing the line at making a pilgrimage to Orchard House).

Our girl Audrey knew a thing or two about the benefits of hard work and overcoming adversity as well. Before making her way as a prima ballerina and becoming one of the most celebrated actresses of all time, Hepburn was a World War II survivor. During the Nazi occupation of the Netherlands, she experienced extreme hardship; her brother went to a labor camp in Germany for a while and her own uncle and cousin were shot. Her family was forced to resort to making flour out of tulip bulbs to bake cakes and biscuits. But rather than becoming bitter, she said, "Our past has made us what we are today. Your soul is nourished by all your experiences."[15] She went on to work with UNICEF and gave much back to the children of the world who were in need as she once was.

Someday you will have your own success story. Perhaps you're building it right now. The experiences you've gained and the lessons you're learning will all help you become who you're supposed to be. So rather than shying away from toil and hard work, embrace them. Let them challenge you and spur you on to become an even better version of yourself.

If you ever start to doubt, remind yourself of your original dream and goal—it will keep you motivated and inspired, even when the going gets tough. See yourself already standing on that Olympic podium, receiving the Nobel Prize, or opening your own business. Whatever your goal is, it's not unattainable. Even if you don't have renowned 'rents or gobs of cash, you can make it happen anyway. In the end, the success will be sweeter, the payoff bigger, the—well, you get the point. You're perfectly suited and fully equipped to turn your dream into a reality. Go make it happen!

*Chapter Six*

# Choose Your Friends Wisely

"Show me your friends and I'll show you your future."
—*Author unknown*

Elizabeth and Jane Bennett. Tina Fey and Amy Poehler. Monica and Rachel. These were some famous friendships. Friends sometimes get a bad rap for being unreliable or fickle, but I would suggest that the majority of friendships are faithful, supportive, and consistent. These are the relationships that have the potential to see you through some of the biggest accomplishments and biggest failures of your life—some of the biggest joys and biggest disappointments. Through new boyfriends, breakups, births, deaths— the good ones will be there, no matter what. It's no secret that friends can have an incredible impact on our lives—for the better or for the worse. Apparently that's why our parents always said, "Choose your friends wisely!"

I think one of the sweetest examples of friendship I've ever heard came a few years back, when I was asked to speak at a summer convention in Virginia. One of the group's notable alumni addressed the group that night and gave a powerful illustration of the impact that friendships can have. She began to tell of how her father had passed away when she was in college. It was a very difficult time, but when she looked out at everyone who had gathered for the funeral, she saw rows and rows of her fellow sorority sisters, all there to support her in her time of need. She didn't even know some of them, but their show of support made an indelible impact on her young life.

Friends can make all the difference in the world. I love that Courteney Cox and Jennifer Aniston have maintained their *Friends* bond to this day, Sophie Turner and Maisie Williams got subtle matching tattoos of the date they learned they'd be playing the Stark sisters on *Game of Thrones*, and real-life besties Candace Cameron Bure and Andrea Barber have recently had a revival of fun-loving D.J.-and-Kimmy shenanigans. Friends can be lifelong assets and blessings. It only makes sense to want good ones. Take stock of your current relationships. Do they uplift you and encourage you? Are they dragging you down? Surround yourself with people who have your best in mind.

It's no secret that future employers are now Facebooking potential clients, scrolling through their friends lists and making assessments based on first-mouse-click impressions. Too many late-night party pics or profanity-laced comments could mean the difference between your scoring that dream job and heading back home to crash with your parents (my poor mother, I've lived with her for a total of three *years* post-college). Your posse crashing a work event could mean the end of a job. Even the sororities you belong to could conjure up all kinds of opinions from potential friends and bosses. Your circles of friends have more influence than you might think.

Relationships in general are a really big deal. Think about it. Life is entirely made up of the conversations, friendships, memories, meetings, fights, secrets, jokes, and experiences we gather from those around us. When our moms call to check in, they give the status report on our old friends and family members. We come home from work and talk about our inter-actions with others. We make plans to deliberately leave the house and see specific people of interest to us. My daughter said it best when she was four: "A party is when you go do something with all the people you usually go do something with." What would we do without relationships? Who would we share our big news with? Where would we go for a good cry? A friendless life would be a sad existence.

We don't usually start out the first day of kindergarten pon-dering the fact that we're going to be confronted with many choices of friends, and that the ones we pick could possibly shape our entire existence. No, friends just seem to happen (at least until later in life, when you're either uprooted by a family move or plopped into a freshman dormitory and forced to become fast friends with the nearest female who likes the same sitcoms and bathes regularly). But as we get older and begin making conscious, deliberate acquaintance choices, things get tricky. The friends we choose will be the ones who walk with us through new boyfriends, new jobs, family crises, grad school, marriage, babies, bad breakups, and really bad haircuts. If these "friends" don't support and encourage us, it might be time to seek out some new ones.

How do we go about finding and keeping those really great friends? We can start by surrounding ourselves with positive people. And no, that doesn't mean you specifically need to run out and make nice with that really perky girl who gets into work at 4 a.m. every day, or the one at the gym whose pony-tail bounces higher than the length of her head. You just need to seek out others who will encourage you when you're hav-ing a bad day and, perhaps more importantly, cheer you on when you're having a really *great* day (I think we ladies are the only species on the planet that befriends others when they're down and out and then turns into a jealous bobcat the minute the other one starts to succeed). A true friend is the one who will be there to congratulate you when you win an Academy Award and who was also there to hold your hair back when you were puking your guts out in the bathroom stall two hours before from sheer nerves! So keep your eyes peeled for the hair-holding kind.

As cliché as it may sound, finding someone who's a good listener is also a necessity in friendship. Anyone can speak, but it takes intelligence, self-control, and maturity to set our own interests aside and focus our attention on the needs and concerns of someone else for a change. Not only is it hard to feel validated in a relationship where you can't get a word in edgewise, it's just not a lot of fun. A good friendship is built on the mutual sharing of ideas, dreams, concerns, and fears. If we find ourselves on the short end of the sharing stick, it might be difficult to keep the friendship going. And one way we can learn to identify a good listener is by being a great one ourselves.

We can start by asking about our friend's day and then shutting up. We can inquire about our coworker's weekend and then just let him talk about it. Or we can simply stop fiddling with our phones long enough to make eye contact and let the person we're talking to know that we're genuinely interested in hearing what they have to say. In our drive-up, fly-by, fast-talking society, listening is a lost art. But I'm convinced that we can be the ones to bring it back.

The importance of listening also extends beyond close personal friendships—it's a crucial aspect of success. It's no secret that employers relish discovering an employee who does something right the first time, and you can chalk that up to being a good listener. No one wants to have to repeat instructions or directions twice, so sitting up and paying attention will take you further. I've learned the hard way the imperativeness of tuning in to what others are saying. I once had a radio interview with a station in Australia; I think phone interviews can be difficult anyway just due to the nature of the medium— dropped calls, static, garbled words, and so on, but this one was particularly tricky because there were at least two radio personalities on the call and I was having a hard time distinguishing their voices—one would ask a question and I wasn't sure if the speaker was directing it at me or the other person. The group began discussing an Audrey Hepburn movie and asked my opinion, but I had a hard time making out the question and had to ask them twice to repeat it. To make matters worse, my phone cut off—in the middle of the live interview. I immediately tried to call back into the station, but by the time I got connected back to the hosts they had gone to commercial break and had to squeeze me in later. I felt so bad! I should have been more prepared and asked them beforehand what format the interview would take and found a location with better phone service. You live and learn.

It also doesn't hurt to make a valiant attempt to remember names and faces during introductions and casual meetings. One of my friends was actually introduced to someone *fourteen* times before he remembered her. Granted, some people simply have more observant personalities than others (e.g., my husband). He practically has a photographic memory—he can tell you exactly which seat so-and-so sat in during fourth grade and what I ordered at that Greek restaurant nine years go. And yet he can't match up a pair of socks to save his life. Intriguing. Anyway, after we leave an event, he has to give me a debriefing of everyone I met and talked to. "The girl with brown hair was Amber—she introduced herself to you, remember? Then you talked to Chris and his wife after that. She told you her name was Carly; did you catch that?" I can usually remember the conversation that we had and any stories they told me; it simply takes me two or three times to commit their names to memory. If you see someone you should know but have a slipup and can't remember, just be honest and let them know you remember them, but you're drawing a blank on their name. It doesn't hurt to remind them of your name, either—maybe they're just as bad with names as you are. They will appreciate the effort and the honesty; personally, I would prefer to have to remind someone several times of my name than be ignored altogether. And again, some brains are just better wired for this than others, but we can all still make an effort.

If we're going to go anywhere in life, it's also essential to surround ourselves with friends who have admirable habits and minor vices—those who will help us kick our own harmful habits, not just drag us down into the mire with them and theirs. I've been amazed at the honesty and vulnerability of many girls who come to see me at a book event, or chat afterward at the signing table about problems or issues in their lives—I've heard unbelievable stories (both victorious and heartbreaking) and feel so humbled and privileged that they would open up to me. I count it as an honor to be thought of as a sister figure of sorts, and I don't take that lightly. So, first of all, I'd like to let you know that whatever you're going through, *you're not alone.* Someone has been there, survived it, and lived to tell the tale. And second, if you're walking through a hard time or struggling with an issue of some sort,

I'd like to offer you some encouragement. Clearly, I'm not a licensed counselor or therapist of any sort, just someone who's talked to lots and lots of girls. I've seen and heard it all, and nothing scares or shocks me. So if you're worried that your problem is too big, too overwhelming, too scary, or too heavy to share with someone, think again. The best part of my job is hearing your stories—that includes the good, the bad, and the ugly. Therefore, if you're needing guidance or encouragement in a certain area, read on.

If you're struggling with self-image and potential eating-disorder thoughts, find some supportive friends who will take you to counseling and not care if you're a size 2 or a size 10. It's probably not helpful if your bestie just had cardboard and cigarettes for lunch, so find a support group or a local chapter that will discuss healthy cooking and food choices. Your local Whole Foods can be a great resource for finding like-minded groups of health-conscious individuals. If you feel that you need more help than a cooking class can offer, check out your local church—many times they offer free counseling and teaching for people trying to kick an addictive lifestyle.

If you're trying to get sober, be sure to surround yourself with solid, trustworthy people, rather than your usual group of drinking buddies and barhopping cronies. Find a friend who will go with you to AA, or start attending a support group at your local church. When Vicki Vodka comes calling, wanting you to do shots over at her house again, it will be a lot easier to say no when you've got a group of supportive peeps waiting on the other line to go see a movie or eat out at that new restaurant. If you want to get off drugs, look into a rehabilitation center or medical facility with a good drug treatment program. Then get rid of that old contact list and make it a point to seek out new friends who will support you in your new lifestyle, not drag you back into your old ways.

For those struggling with depression, anxiety, or mental illness, just knowing that you're not alone and that someone cares about you can be a huge help. Beyond that, knowing that you can and WILL get better is a huge hurdle to cross. The truth is, you *can* get better. But constantly talking with friends who are negative about life themselves can cause a downward spiral. Find someone—preferably an authority figure—who can help you see past the cloud of gloom in front of you. Seek out a counselor from a local church or hospital and take it day by day. There's still sunshine behind those clouds, and you will see it again.

Have you found yourself unexpectedly pregnant? Pregnancy can be daunting, overwhelming, and terrifying—and that's *with* a supportive partner! I know it's scary to imagine bringing a baby into this world, but let me tell you, it can be the best thing that will ever happen to you. If you decide to give the baby up for adoption, you'll be creating a better life for that little person and some lucky family will be blessed to raise him or her. Before you do anything drastic, seek wisdom, guidance, and support. There are lots of great organizations that will give you and your baby resources, medical attention, counseling, and a fresh start. It's never too late to ask for help.

Despite what medical diagnosis you've been given, what pills you're currently taking, or what mess you've gotten yourself into, you can be free from the darkness that you're living in. You're bigger than your situation. You were made for great things, so don't let this little bump in the road derail you. It's just life—we've all made mistakes and no one is any better, or any worse, than anyone else. Don't let fear and isolation keep you from moving forward. You will never regret the decision to take care of yourself and your health. Even if you feel like this is the end, remember that it might actually be just the beginning.

By the way, these are no small things to overcome. (In fact, they're huge. If you're taking a step right now in the right direction, we are rooting for you and your breakthrough!) It's imperative to not only create a healthy physical environment for yourself *now*, but also to establish an extended network of supportive family and friends for *after*. And if you know someone who is going through a tough time or dealing with one of the aforementioned issues, be the friend they need right now. Encourage your friend to get help and be there to champion their recovery and cheer them on to the finish line. It's a pretty sweet view once they get there.

Maybe you're just trying to have a better outlook on life. It's easy to get sucked into a negative mind-set if those around us are gossips, critics, and pessimists. Debbie Downer from down the hall will probably not help the situation; instead, seek out optimistic and confident friends who will keep you upbeat. Are you attempting to buckle down and study for grad school? Let your usual festivity-planning group know that you're not up for late nights anymore, but you would love to hang out during the day. Trying to pay off credit card debt? Find some friends who will be fine with low-budget fun for a while. Make it fun by clipping coupons, grocery shopping in pairs, and then cooking a meal together. You'll save dough and still be able to socialize. To sum up, we need friends who will support us in our endeavors and, furthermore, friends who will look us in the eye and tell us when we need to get help rather than simply ignore, or even encourage, the problem.

Of course, getting rid of dead weight can be easier said than done. Some of these bad relationships have been with us for years, and it's hard to simply shake them off. The queen of hip-hop soul, Mary J. Blige, had such an experience and successfully broke free of her dark past. Of that life-changing moment, she says, "People I thought were friends were just dispersing. I could feel myself slipping away too. And I thought, 'I don't want to slip away because of alcohol and drugs and loneliness.'"[16]

You can have the same success story; be brutally honest with your close inner circle and extend an invitation for them to change along with you. Invite them to AA, find new hangouts away from the clubs, keep one another accountable. It may be difficult for them to understand in the beginning, but after a while, if they don't support your new goals and life-style, you can and should, with no regrets, amicably tell them it's time to part ways.

Besides supportiveness and being considerate, a hefty dose of humor is a key component of any good relationship. If we don't have someone to laugh with about mistakes, boys, and obnoxious coworkers, things can get pretty boring. Clearly, I'm no doctor, and I am by no means offering precise medical stats here, but I have heard that laughter might help stimulate our heart and circulatory system and can actually improve job performance. Perhaps we should all take a ten-minute break and just laugh. The now-famous *Chewbacca Mom* video quickly went viral (over 137 million views to date), and when asked about the reason for its popularity, the video's star, Candace Payne, said, "The world, as a whole, is in need of a good laugh."[17] I couldn't agree more.

If you need to kick-start the comical in your relationships, check out *I Like You* by Sandol Stoddard Warburg. My two best friends and I discovered this tiny red children's book at a store in New York City, and we bought one another copies because it is flawlessly endearing and entertaining. We deemed that each of us could give it away to only one other person in life—the guy we decided to marry. Consequently, this humorous little book is sacred among our circle, and I would highly recommend picking up a couple of copies for you and your crew, too.

Still at a loss for the amusing? The following is a brief list of entertaining outings and ideas for us and our witty broods to partake in the next time we get bored.

- Buy tickets to see a play—find the nearest Broadway tour headed your way. Even if it's a local children's theater production, it's so much fun to see kids' reactions and relive childhood tales and stories.
- Bake cookies with whatever ingredients you have left in the cupboards. I've actually consumed ramen chicken-noodle cookies before. They were dry.
- Buy a ten-dollar kiddie pool at Walmart and throw a "pool" party. Hand out sunscreen and invite a designated "lifeguard" to hang up signs all over that read "No Diving."
- Rent old episodes of *I Love Lucy*—specifically, the chocolate-factory episode.
- Get makeovers from the Clinique counter at the mall. Enough said.
- Three words: *Black. Light. Bowling.*
- Get cheap-seat tickets to a local minor-league baseball game. Check beforehand for special deals like dollar hot dogs or free hat night.
- Play Apples to Apples or Taboo—and invite your parents.
- Host a themed party: Christmas in July; Saved by the Bell, 2003 (bring your old iPod and put together a mix completely made up of tunes from that year).
- Hit thrift stores and assemble your next going-out getup entirely from your findings—my husband played guitar in

a hilarious and short-lived '80s cover band, and he actually wore some snakeskin pants from Salvation Army during one of their shows. *That* is what I call repurposing.

Now that we know what to look for in friends, how do we keep them? I'm sure we've all experienced the friendship that starts out great but then goes to pot after one person moves away, gets hitched, or undergoes a job transfer (all of which are inevitably followed by various promises to "definitely" keep in touch). Or perhaps some of our long-lost friends are still close by but simply too busy to maintain a relationship. It's hard to keep up when time, distance, and new relationships get in the way. The thing that counts is effort as far as I'm concerned. Even if you get to see each other only once in a blue moon, or talk on the phone once a year, it's the thought that counts. Just the fact that you called or texted might mean the world.

My sister is the absolute best at this. She is hands down the most giving and thoughtful person I've ever known; she makes me want to be a better friend and human being. One day she had a bouquet of yellow daisies delivered to me at work, just because. Another time, I came home to a FedEx package on my doorstep—she had found a T-shirt that Rory wore on an episode of *Gilmore Girls* and bought it for me just for fun. And when she lived in New York City, she would send me all kinds of fun NYC-themed goodies. If we all followed the Abby Practice of Giving, our friends would never leave our side!

But what if we're strapped for cash? We definitely don't have to go out and lay down gobs of green to show our friends that we value them; there are plenty of pocketbook-friendly ways to spread the love. Awhile back, I received a note in the mail from an old friend that completely made my day, and it required only the chump change to cover the cost of the stamp. Even if you're not a big pen-and-paper person, never underestimate the power of a phone call, a random postcard, or even a thoughtful e-mail. Nowadays we rely so heavily on our news feed to keep us abreast of friends' lives—it's worth it to do something thoughtful *off-line*. We could assemble a recipe book of a friend's favorite dishes by simply printing them off or handwriting some cute recipe cards. Or surprise her with takeout from her favorite restaurant. I'm still a little sad that no one uses CDs anymore; otherwise, I would suggest making your friend a good old-fashioned mix!

On the off chance that we do have a couple of bucks to spare, we could send a bag of our best friend's favorite candy to work when she gets that raise, or surprise our sister-in-law with a Saturday afternoon of prepaid mani-pedis (thank you, Hannah). Or take a cue from Abby and find quirky paraphernalia from your friend's favorite movie or sitcom. Another great (and cheap) little gesture is to treat your friend at your local ice cream shop. It's imperative to walk there together and get in some quality talk time. Not only will both parties benefit from the time spent together during a random act of kindness, but the act of giving something away seems to elicit a sort of natural high.

Another great way to maintain a healthy friendship is to have a regularly scheduled date. Even though we lived together, my old roommate and I had a designated ritual of eating popcorn for dinner and watching a movie every Sunday night. We set aside other obligations and assignments and always tried to make that "us" time. You rarely get to talk about personal things with friends at the office, even though you see each other all day long, so consider taking a brief break to walk around the building or go on a quick coffee run together somewhere nearby. Find a place that works for both parties and make a concrete decision to meet up every week, regardless of outside obligations or circumstances (exceptions may be made for emergencies involving oozing blood or exposed internal organs).

You can also try setting goals together. Two friends of mine, Robin and Whitney, wanted to train for a marathon and decided to run together every single morning (I can say with near certainty that I have not run twenty-six miles in my entire life combined). They consequently developed a close bond and still work out together every morning. Do you have a workout goal in mind? Want to join a gym? Call up a friend/accountability partner—that will make everything way more enjoyable and force you to keep going and push yourself a little harder even when you're tired.

A couple of my other friends were both trying for acceptance into highly competitive graduate programs and decided to set a daily study goal together. Besides being accepted, they both had a great time and would order takeout and meet at fun, different locations to crack open the books. If you and another groupie are both aiming to get into law school, med school, or just a summer learning program, develop a study schedule together to make sure you're prepped for the LSAT, MCAT, or any other kind of AT.

If you have several friends who are passionate about the same cause, why not plan an event to raise money and awareness? My friend Kenny loved TOMS shoes, and he personally organized a Christmas party for a bunch of us to get together and decorate blank shoes to give to people in need. A couple of my other friends supported World Vision children, and we would always try to brainstorm about new things we could send to "our kids" for birthdays and holidays. Another great organization, She's the First (www.shesthefirst.org), gives you various options for getting involved (Host a tie-dye cupcake bake sale! Sweat for STF through races or fitness classes!) to ultimately make a difference in the lives of girls around the world. Find common areas of passion and ideals with other people and watch those friendships blossom.

I'm an innate people pleaser, which makes it hard to say no. To anything. But if there's a certain someone you feel not-so-great about spending time with, don't beat yourself up about turning down a social invitation every once in a while. It's your life, which means *you* get to choose your friends. We're all adults here, and if we're finding ourselves investing in acquaintances that are dead weight, we shouldn't be afraid to politely excuse ourselves from the relationship. This obviously doesn't have to be a ruthless or cruel process: Simply let the person know that you're busy trying to keep up with the demands of life and need to set some boundaries and priorities.

Extreme cases of accidentally taking on a fanatical friend are rare, but they do indeed happen. These situations can be hard to navigate because you don't want to risk ruining your rapport, but, sometimes, the practical details of the relationship just don't work for one party or the other. I am *the worst* at this. I typically avoid conflict like the plague, so I don't exactly relish the thought of having to decline a friendship. Case in point: Several years ago, a new girl started at the job where I was working and immediately asked me for my cell number about an hour after she clocked in. I thought that was a little enthusiastic but naively assumed she was just attempting to get to know everyone. She called my cell phone at 6:45 the next morning, asking if I wanted to go get breakfast with her. I knew right then and there that I was not dealing with the average eager beaver.

I politely declined any more early-morning invites and informed her that I actually ate breakfast with my husband every morning at home. Later that week, I became slightly concerned when she approached my desk and asked me to buy a gym membership with her. When she called again the next week asking if I wanted to help her make homemade Christmas ornaments, plan a dinner party, and then go for a four-mile hike afterward, I knew I had to put the kibosh on the situation.

That was a horribly difficult thing for me to do, as confrontation is not my strong suit. It's like ripping off a Band-Aid—it's not pretty, but you just have to do it. There are certain relationships that call for us to set some ground rules. I think the key is finding a way to firmly and decisively let the person know your status without personally offending him or her. Christmas Hiker Breakfast Girl was actually really sweet. I got along great with her at work. But on top of my forty-plus hours at the office, I was finishing college at night and doing some freelance writing on the weekends, so the truth was, I didn't have a lot of spare time before or after work. And any extra time that I did have, I wanted to spend with my husband, as we were newlyweds. I finally had to inform her that I had lots of things to juggle between work, family, school, and writing, and unfortunately didn't have time for a lot of outside activities. Luckily, she got the hint and we were then able to peacefully coexist at the office as normal coworkers.

If you're stuck in a sticky situation, carefully lay out an exit plan and then execute it tactfully. Especially if it's someone you see on a daily basis. You don't have to go so far as to cut them out completely. Just find a way to let them know that you value them but aren't able to dedicate a lot of time to the relationship right now. Anyone should be able to understand that.

See, that wasn't so bad, was it?

Now that we have an established circle of great girlfriends, it's all too easy to get stuck in a rut when it comes to activities. Do you find yourselves going to the same old hangouts? Eating the same Chinese takeout? Watching the same shows every week? My two best friends discovered the perfect cure for relationship-rut blues. We each took a fun online quiz to help us discover our signature cities and made it a point to visit all three before we were out of college. It was the most fun we'd ever had! If you and your gang are up for the challenge, google "signature city" and "quiz" and go crazy.

To further enhance newfound good-friend habits, here is a slew of out-of-the-box ideas for friends everywhere to enjoy together. This should keep you from being bored for quite some time!

&#10086; Grab your favorite lunch, then meet up at the park for a picnic.
&#10086; Sign up for Pilates, Zumba, or any other group fitness course.
&#10086; Take salsa-dancing lessons together every week.
&#10086; Hit the local farmers' market and make an organic dinner afterward.

❀ Clean out your closets together and make a donation to Goodwill.

❀ Take a weekend road trip to a randomly selected city.

❀ Schedule an old-movie marathon.

❀ Register for a BYOB paint class—most cities have scores of them these days.

❀ Volunteer at a local animal shelter or a nonprofit one Saturday a month.

❀ Take random pics, print them, and host a scrapbooking party.

❀ Paint each other's bedrooms a new color.

❀ Start your own book club.

❀ Meet up at the local "movie in the park" night.

❀ Host a progressive dinner.

❀ Schedule a pedicure together over lunch breaks.

❀ Save up for VIP concert tickets to see your favorite artist.

❀ Take a pottery class and make your own coffee mugs.

❀ Check out your local library's reading programs, then volunteer to read to kids together.

It's important to note that we absolutely need friends (good ones, that is). My mom has always been more than just a mom to me—she's my best friend, and I don't know what I would do without her. I still obnoxiously call her every single day. My sister and I are extremely close, too; I consider her to be my other best friend, and I get seriously sad if I go for more than a few days without seeing her—and that's the way it should be, right? Whether or not it's our family that provides a friend-ship support system, we just need to make sure we have two or three close friends we can count on, no matter what.

When you surround yourself with uplifting and like-minded comrades, life is just easier to handle. Everything becomes more fun, and challenges become easier to face. It's always heartening to have someone you can call on the phone for no good reason whatsoever, someone who won't mind if you shoot chocolate milk out your nose while you're laughing, and someone who'll listen and just let you cry when you've had the worst day of your life. If you don't have friends like that, it's time to find new ones—friends who will make your life fun, healthy, and well-rounded.

*Chapter Seven*

# Let Him Come Calling

"It's all any of us wants—to find a nice person to hang
out with 'til we drop dead. Not a lot to ask!"
—*Lorelai Gilmore*[18]

I t seems like such a simple thing, right? Boy meets girl.
Girl meets boy. They fall in love. He picks out a ring. She
picks out a dress. And they live happily ever after. But
judging by all the cards, commercials, campaigns, and ad
dollars, there must be more to it than just initial attraction.
If it were easy to find a soul mate, a good chunk of reality TV
today would cease to exist. Entire self-help sections would
come crumbling down, and the chick-flick genre would all but
dry up. There must be a sort of intangible, stars-have-aligned,
divine power at work—otherwise, everyone would just settle
for the first remotely attractive person of the opposite sex they
happened to meet. And we all know *that* didn't happen. (I still
have the cringe-worthy letter I wrote to my crush in eighth
grade to prove it.) The amazing thing is that we all want the
same thing—whether you're fourteen and wishing that cute
skater boy would turn around and notice you in class, or

123

thirty-four and mouse-clicking profiles daily, wondering if you'll ever find Mr. Right—we all just want someone to love. And isn't that the hope of all humanity, really? Think about it: The richest of the rich get married. The poorest of the poor get married. Pro athletes get married. Dentists get married. Guys digging ditches get married. So clearly it's a basic desire of almost all civilization. With it being such an innate aspiration, you'd think we'd have it down to a science by now. And yet here we are, still discussing how little we know about it.

Well, let me rephrase that—we do know something: We know what we want. We want tall, athletic, handsome, charming, witty, rich, smart, kind, good with our friends, nice to our mom, et cetera. We just don't know how to go about getting it. My seventh-grade self was so convinced that I knew exactly what I wanted that I made a list. It was a bizarre, obscure list, mind you, but a list nevertheless. I prayed that God would somehow figure out the right guy for me, and could he please meet all of the following requirements?

1. He has to like *Seinfeld*.
2. He has to play guitar.
3. He has to be taller than me.

That was it. I figured the shorter I kept the list, the better my odds were. Don't ask why I thought those things were imperative to a relationship, but the odd thing is that my husband fits all those ridiculous stipulations. He was the first person I met who came to college with a stack of *Seinfeld* DVDs, he played electric guitar in a pop/rock band, and he's a good four inches taller than me. I know that may seem like a silly mash-up of absurdities and kismet, but for my young heart, it was proof that God had known what I needed and wanted since day one.

It can be hard to wait, though, when you've got your "Perfect Guy" list and are all set to book the Plaza. Especially when it appears as though jumping from partner to partner and sending X-rated texts are the only ways to get what you want. I have no judgment against such things, but if you're not comfortable with those methods, dating can seem a little disconcerting. Well, I happen to have good news for you: Those aren't the only ways to get what you want. Sure, those things are common occurrences but not for everyone, and they're certainly not requirements for finding a boyfriend or future husband. There are amazing guys out there who are willing to wait for you, so don't feel pressured to do anything other than be yourself.

Another good reason not to go with the flow is because it doesn't generally work—at least not if your goal is a lasting, committed, healthy relationship. Why? Well, I didn't make the rules, so I don't really know why; it just doesn't. If I had figured out the makeup of the male mind, I would be writing a different book. But there *are* some time-honored traditions and practices that seem to be the trademarks of every long-lasting relationship. What are they? The first, I feel, is the art of making yourself available but not too accessible.

What does that mean? Being available, but not too accessible? Well, being available is easy—just show up. Be your cute, usual self wherever you go and guys will pick up on the fact that you're available. Not too difficult. The second part, not being too accessible, is where we usually get into trouble. But how is being too accessible bad? Well, by "being too accessible," I mean "freaking-him-out-by-never-leaving-his-side."

In no particular order, we have the following means of scaring off a new guy: posting, liking, e-mailing, messaging, stalking, texting, tweeting, calling, showing up unannounced, inviting him over, and did I mention coming on too strong? We will talk about why being so accessible is nothing but a curse, but first, why do we even care so much to begin with?

It's no secret that we girls start fantasizing about a fairy-tale wedding and happily-ever-after love story around the same time we start teething. Relationships are a big deal to us. We want to hear all about our roommate's new boyfriend, have to get every detail of our coworker's upcoming nuptials, and lament the latest celebrity It Couple breakup. We love to watch TLC's *Married at First Sight*, feverishly scan *Us Weekly* for the latest blossoming celebrity romance, and sob every time we see *Cinderella*. We spend hours prepping ourselves for a date and even more time obsessing about what our potential children will look like and whether or not our initials mesh nicely. Conclusion: Girls love love.

Over two thousand years ago, King Solomon wrote an entire book dedicated to love, which just goes to show you that this whole love-romance-dating thing has been going on a long time, and we're probably not going to be the ones to change the entire course of it anytime soon.

*You've captured my heart, dear friend. You looked at me, and I fell in love. One look my way and I was hopelessly in love!*
—Song of Songs 4:8–9 (MSG)

Here we have the entire saga of love and romance summed up in a few phrases: guy meets girl, guy falls in love with girl, guy can't think of anyone but her and is obsessed with girl up until dying day à la *The Notebook*. This age-old plot could explain the rapid popularity of said movie. I know all of us ladies love that love story, and as much as they might grumble, deep down, guys like the movie, too (even my husband, who has a beard, drives a truck, and aspires to be a lumberjack). Why? Because it is, without a doubt, the ideal illustration of romance: Guys want a girl to chase after, and girls want a guy to want to track them down.

This, at first, would seem to fly in the face of twenty-first-century feminism and our girls-rock mentality. But really, it doesn't. I would argue that the heart of feminism is the desire to be respected and seen as an equal—if you're desiring to have a guy respect you, the best way is to show him you're worthy of respect. Make him work for you! You're worth the work. If you're desiring to be seen as an equal, show him that you're intelligent and discerning, and that you're not going to settle for a cheap relationship built on one-night stands and booty calls. Instead, build that relationship on meaningful conversations and fun experiences with your family and friends. If he's a winner, he will gladly jump through any and all hoops you put up for him.

It has always been this way—from Adam and Eve to knights climbing the tower for their ladies-in-waiting to Jane Austen's generation of gallant gentlemen writing letters to their intended, right up to our reality-obsessed era of *Arranged*. Guys still want to pursue the girl, and no amount of texts, uncensored videos, or Facebook posts is going to change that. I'm not sure why we've all of a sudden taken it upon ourselves to change the structural makeup of a guy's mind, but I'm telling you right now, it's pointless. The implementation of the Sadie Hawkins dance in 1937 didn't do anything to alter the ingrained behaviors of guys and girls. I'm serious—the best thing you can do is simply *let him be the guy.* And what do guys want to do? Chase things!

Men are natural-born hunters—they like the thrill of the chase. They race cars, bid on worthless eBay junk, and go hunting in the woods. They love a good pursuit. (I realize that girls can do all these things, too; I'm simply speaking in generalities. I love football and trapshooting and a myriad of other male-dominated activities as well.) Even when we were young, most of the boys were out playing cops and robbers while we girls jumped rope. They'd scale the tree fort with sticks and rocks for a good sniper position while we girls taught each other line dances and braided each other's hair. Again, I'm not saying that girls can't do all those things, because they *can*. But in general, it's in boys' natures to hunt, chase, and track down, and if you make yourself readily available (calling, texting, stalking), guys no longer have anything to pursue. And if there's nothing there to chase after, dream about, or hunt down, they've probably already lost interest.

So why would we subconsciously sabotage all those efforts through our modern-day attempts at finding true love? I've done a lot of idiotic things in the name of love myself, so don't worry, I'm not judging. But the problem still remains. I'd like to think that it's out of sheer naïveté—most of us aren't in a lucid mental state when throwing ourselves at our crush; we aren't the least bit aware that we are actually driving that poor boy further away.

I had a sweet friend who was devastated by a particular boy's lack of interest in her advances. She tried everything to get his attention—even offering to drive to his house and make him dinner—but he continually made excuses to avoid her, usually stating that he needed to study all weekend and wouldn't be available. It became clear that she was putting way too much energy into a clearly one-sided relationship and finally moved on. But it was hard to see the big red flags he was throwing when she was in the middle of a crush. His excuses all seemed quite reasonable when she was head over heels. But in cases like this, the sooner a girl gets the hint, the sooner she can get on with her life.

And lest you think I've got it all together, I have a personal tale of shame when it comes to indifferent crushes. I had been somewhat interested in a guy for several months and tried to furtively arrange occasions where I could run into him. One night, I stealthily tried to get on his team during a game of kickball, and when that didn't work, I thought I could try to at least play *near* him. Well, he ended up *breaking my arm* during the game and didn't even stop playing to say he was sorry, even after I came back with a cast on. So much for all my romantic planning and plotting! Clearly, he was not interested. I finally got the message and moved on.

The sad thing is, we usually think our sly attempts at catching a guy's attention are coy and ambiguous, when in fact, they are obvious and palpable. We think we're simply sending smiley texts, periodically posting insinuating Bruno Mars lyrics, and nonchalantly floating near his desk, but he sees all those things and reads: *Warning! This girl wants to marry me!*

What are the warning signs that you're venturing into stalker territory? Well, first of all, I could have saved myself a lot of grief if *He's Just Not That into You* had been published while I was still in high school. But beyond that, the first clue that any potential-boyfriend scenario should be stopped in its tracks is if *you're* always having to call *him*. Next, any "Friday night studying" excuses or any other kind of unnatural reasoning coming from him should immediately tip you off (yes, there are the occasional finals or semester test situations, but the majority of the time, a guy who's interested would rather be with *you*). If you still haven't gotten the clue, any "Thanks, but no thanks" responses should indicate that you've crossed the line into desperate-weird-crazy territory. And finally, the "I just want to be friends" speech is pretty much the nail in any relationship's proverbial coffin.

That being said, relationships are hard to navigate at any stage—and when you add in attributes like clingy, smothering, and no self-awareness, things can really get messy. When it comes to the opposite gender, everything seems like a big mystery. *Does he like me? Do I like him? What am I going to do if he does like me?* We've all made foolish mistakes in this department, so I've got no stones to throw—relationships are tricky and take a lot of work. And that's on a good day. Not to mention, I can see it from both angles—I've been the starry-eyed girl, hoping and praying that he'll notice me; I've also had a lot of guy friends tell me it's no fun to be the object of obsessive behavior. Why does love have to be so hard?! No matter, it *is* possible and strongly Jordan-recommended to keep that self-respect intact by not begging for affection. Because the truth is, you were okay before you met him, and you'll be okay without him. You don't need to lower your standards by becoming embarrassingly desperate. And if you think that guys can't tell...well, apparently they can.

One of my good guy friends was the object of every girl's desire. He was one of those dark-haired, blue-eyed, naturally tan specimens who attracted girls for miles. I always found it a comical scene and was especially intrigued by the fact that he never showed real interest in any of them. So one day over lunch, I finally decided to broach the subject.

"Why don't you ever date one of these girls?" I inquired.

"What girls?" he asked cluelessly as he dug into his salad.

"What girls? Oh, just the horde that follows you around drooling and hanging on your every word," I replied.

"Ohhh, *those* girls. Well, I don't like any of them," he stated matter-of-factly and went back to shoveling in ranch-covered romaine.

"Why not? They're all obviously in love with *you*."

"Well, that's kind of the problem." He shrugged in a non-helpful, that's-the-way-it-is manner.

"Why is that a problem? Don't you want a girl that's interested in you?"

"Well, yeah, but they're beyond interested. They're like, really into me. And that's not fun for a guy. You want a girl that makes you work for it a little bit. We kinda like the chase."

Aha! A lightbulb went on in my head that day. Boys *can* tell. And it's almost the opposite of what we've been told as women—that if we really put the pedal to the metal, we can get what we want, which is true in a lot of ways. But when it comes to boys, it would appear that putting on the brakes would actually serve us better. Author, counselor, and all-around guy expert John Eldredge says, "Deep in his heart, every man longs for a battle to fight, an adventure to live, and a beauty to rescue."[19] (By the way, if you want a good gift for your guy, look no further than John's book *Wild at Heart: Discovering the Secret of a Man's Soul.*)

This is good news! It means there's some guy out there who's willing to climb the tower and fight off the dragon to get to you. He may be a little rough around the edges (if I allowed Drew to decorate our house, I'm convinced he would decorate it with guns and Cheetos), but I always say—he doesn't need to be perfect, he just needs to be perfect for *you*. The aforementioned statement is also encouraging because it means we don't need to debase ourselves to get his attention, or compromise our integrity to keep him. Just be you and he'll come calling. Don't get discouraged by the entourage of males who just hooted and hollered at you on the way back from your lunch break, or that creepy guy reading a gross magazine in the store; there are plenty of honorable boys out there. Just keep being your fabulous self and before you know it, you'll find him.

Don't believe me? If you're feeling a bit stubborn and are determined to prove me wrong, that's cool. I know there are exceptions to the rule, and I have no doubt that you can come up with one or two off the top of your head. But as far as the majority of the gender goes, I would guess they're somewhat similar. Just take a gander at the responses to the question I posed to a few delightful, successful, happily married men: Did she pursue you, or did you pursue her? Their answers show that the odds are against those trying to muster up the guts to do the asking first.

**Greg, married forty-two years:** I had to ask Carol. Two of our mutual friends actually tried to set us up on a date, but she refused. So I asked her myself and she finally agreed. We went to a high school basketball game together, and the rest is history.

**José, married four years:** I had to pursue her. I met Tina when we were playing a show at a small club in this obscure town in Alaska. I thought she was the most beautiful girl I'd ever seen, so I started talking to her after the show, asked for her number, and called her first thing the next day.

**Wallace, married nine years:** I definitely had to work to get Leila. She was working as a hostess at a restaurant, so I ended up eating there all the time to get her attention. Eventually, I went out and bought concert tickets to see her favorite band to try and impress her. Apparently it worked.

**Christopher, married twenty-three years:** I initially went after her. I first saw Kerry when our high school football team played her school on a Friday night. She was a cheerleader, she was so cute, and I knew that I just had to say something to her afterward. So I waited around for an hour and a half after the game to talk to her.

**Ryan, married three years:** Natalie came to one of our band's shows with a bunch of her friends; I saw her in the crowd and just knew that I had to go talk to her, so I think you could safely say that I pursued her. I found her afterward, got her number, and haven't stopped talking to her since!

$M$y husband had to do the pursuing as well—I even turned him down twice before agreeing to a date because I thought he was too quiet. He told me later that he was beyond distraught and didn't eat for days because he knew he wanted to marry me but I didn't seem to want to have anything to do with him. Poor guy. Luckily, he mustered up what dignity he had left and asked again, and as it turned out, the third time was the charm.

I'm certainly not anything special, but I still love how my husband finally got my attention. Besides being cute and funny, he is the epitome of a real man who isn't afraid to step up to the plate. Even though he has a naturally shy personality, he found a way to let me know his true feelings. After initially turning him down, I received a real letter in my mailbox from him that said, "Hey, Jordan, I know we just met, but I would really like to get to know you better. I think you're the most fun and amazing girl I've ever met and I'd love to take you out to dinner sometime. I'm going to call you later to see if you'd be okay with that."

Well, that about did it for me. Maybe I've read a few too many Jane Austen novels, but any guy who writes old-fashioned letters scores big points in my book. He then took me to the exact place I had told my sister that I wanted my future husband to take me on our first date, and from that night on, I knew I was going to marry him, too.

Regardless of the guy's current status, bank account, background, or beliefs, if he's interested, he will find a way to let you know. There's no need to interfere with the ways of nature. But I think our fear is that he won't know we're interested. That's why we go to the great lengths we do to make sure he's aware! It's one thing to be on the lookout for a meaningless fling, but it's quite another if you're hoping to meet the One. When the case is the latter, we're generally terrified that he won't pick up on what we're layin' down.

Before you go thinking I'm demanding that everyone throw out their phones and cancel their online dating memberships, think again. Those are tools that can help us find Mr. Right! Rather, it's a matter of *how* you use such media and the vibes you're putting out over the airwaves.

So how do you avoid the clingy-and-desperate act yet still let him know that you're available? It all goes back to not making yourself too accessible. At the onset, it doesn't sound very twenty-first-century-empowered-woman to say this, but in reality, it *is* empowering: You simply need to let him call you (at least for the first time or two). A woman's mystery is one of the biggest attracting factors for a guy. Therefore, when in doubt, just put those phones away, because dialing his digits two hours after you've met is only going to turn him off. In fact, here is a list of activities to abstain from during the initial courting period (which can range from the original meeting to several days or weeks down the road—you'll know this time is over when you both decide to be exclusive).

☐ **Making the initial call**—The only reason to call is if he first calls you and leaves a specific message asking you to call him back. There aren't a lot of exceptions, including "Maybe he lost my number" or "He's really busy, so he probably just forgot" or "He has bad service, so I should just call him." If he was seriously interested in you, he would never lose that number, and even if he did he would find a way to contact you.

☐ **Texting incessantly**—Especially forty-five minutes after you met him to say how much you liked the shirt that he wore tonight. Nothing drains the elusive female mystique faster than a text message that showcases your innermost thoughts and feelings. Leave him to hope, wonder, and get butterflies. Fanatical texting does not leave him wanting more.

☐ **Social network interaction**—Nothing says "overzealous" like an instantaneous Facebook friend request. If he's interested, he will find you. And even after he does, there's no reason to hash out the details of the relationship over social media. If he is truly interested, he will want to talk with and see you in person, so there's no need to spend all your time posting and liking.

☐ **Too-revealing updates**—You need to completely disregard that impulse to race back to your room and blog that you've just met the man of your dreams. Word will inevitably get back to him that you're obsessed, and he'll assume you're a little batty and get completely freaked out. Guys don't want to hear that you're planning their wedding or naming their unborn children (even if you are), so skip the emotional Facebook updates and the tell-all tweets.

☐ **Planting yourself in strategic spots**—The unnatural act of hanging around his hangouts is not only transparent, it's weird. I'm convinced that if you're truly destined to be with someone, you won't have to leave your house at a calculated time, hide out in the bushes for hours, and then magically materialize, looking fresh-faced, surprised to see him, and very available. For the record, driving by his house or apartment multiple times a day doesn't work, either.

Again, once he has lovingly gazed into your eyes and said that he can't imagine himself with anyone else, you're pretty much free to call and text whenever. Until then, the key is to maintain a little mystery. And you can't do that when you're getting a tan from the 24/7 glow of that cell phone, informing him of every minute detail of your day while subtly slipping in hints of matrimony and children. Luckily, by the time he's professed his undying love, he'll be so enamored with you that you won't be able to get rid of him—soon you'll be politely asking him to just leave you alone for a couple of hours so that you can get some actual work done.

Of course, we've all envisioned a happily-ever-after scenario countless times. Since the day we hit puberty and started matching up potential suitors' initials with our own on the back of an Algebra I notebook, we were destined for a lifetime of tear-jerk reactions to every emotionally charged life scenario: harsh breakups, timely Valentine's Day card commercials, long-awaited weddings, every sappy movie in the book...you name it and we're there bawling our eyes out. And frankly, I think that's just fine.

Romance is part of our DNA. If you don't believe me, think back on every good Disney movie. Although humorous supporting characters helped advance the plotlines, most of the major classics essentially involved a girl, a guy, and a happy ending: Belle, Ariel, Jasmine, Anna, Snow White, they're all looking for a good man! So, at an infantile stage, we're already thinking about Prince Charming (I hate to tell you, but sometimes he ends up looking more like the Beast) and wondering exactly how he's going to rescue us, what he'll be wearing, and why on earth he's taking so long to get here. When you add it up, that's a lot of wishing and hoping and praying—from the day we start walking to the day we say "I do."

It's okay to accept that sentimental and hopelessly romantic nature and simply be a girl and let the guys be guys. Pop a bag of popcorn, down a box of chocolates; heck, get a full-body massage and a manicure. Don't be afraid to embrace all of that schmaltzy, gooey, lovey-doveyness. It feels darn good. Sometimes there's only one cure for what ails you—a good chick flick. Need a good cry? Just went through a breakup? Feeling empowered? There's probably a good chick flick for it. Feel free to further indulge your sappy side by consulting the following chick-flick guide according to mood!

If you're feeling jealous ⟶ *Sabrina*

If you're feeling ruthless ⟶ *Love & Friendship*

If you're feeling romantic ⟶ *Only You*

If you feel like laughing ⟶ *My Big Fat Greek Wedding 2*

If you feel destined to be
   together ⟶ *Serendipity*

If you're feeling sappy ⟶ *An Affair to Remember*

If you're feeling homesick ⟶ *The Family Stone*

If you're feeling nostalgic ⟶ *Little Women*

If you're feeling feisty ⟶ *Steel Magnolias*

If you're feeling adventurous ⟶ *Roman Holiday*

If you're feeling your girl
   power ⟶ *Now and Then*

Okay, maybe you're not a hopeless romantic like me and you haven't been pining away for Mr. Right since you were in diapers. You're probably rolling your eyes right now. But you've probably still found yourself baffled by guys and their bewildering actions before, right? Who hasn't? We've all debated and questioned and reasoned and assumed what's going on inside the male mind. Even the most sensible woman can come down with a bad case of cloudy judgment when it comes to men. When he fails to call when he says he will, we tell ourselves, "Well, he *is* really busy with work right now." When he says he doesn't want to commit to the relationship, we tend to rationalize, "Well, he's had really rough relationships in the past." And when he can't call or e-mail for two weeks because he's visiting his parents in Idaho, you hear yourself saying, "Well, he is *really* close to his family." But the truth is that we're all big girls and need to stop waiting, groveling, and pining after someone who is clearly not interested. You can beg, plead, and pray all you want, but if he's not into it, it's probably not going to happen. Once you get it, the signals become easier to read. And the more you heed them, the more dignity you'll retain.

At the heart of things, guys are kind of old-fashioned, too. They want to do the finding, the asking, and the pursuing. If he's not doing any of these and then some, it was probably over before it began. How do you identify these signals and spare yourself the pain and agony? When in doubt, consult the boy-tested-and-approved list below!

💔 **He doesn't call when he says he will:** I don't care if it's three hours or three days later than when he said he was going to call—a guy in love does *not* miss an opportunity to chat with his girl. Period. This pretty much rules out "He might have just lost my number," "He's extra busy with work right now," "He has to get up really early," or "He had other plans tonight." Every guy I've ever spoken with (including my own hubby) says that it doesn't matter how busy they are or who they're with—they'll find a way to call the girl they like.

💔 **He won't commit:** If a guy is in love, he will want to stake his claim. Males are notoriously territorial, and the last thing he would want is another guy moving in on his lady (which should actually make you feel good—you don't want some guy who could not care less if he loses you). Why on earth would you want a guy you have to convince, bribe, and persuade to be with you? No, thanks. If you've been buying into "He just got out of a tough relationship," "He's trying to figure out his life right now," or "He just doesn't want to do the long-distance thing," you can stuff those excuses in a sack and hit the road, because he's obviously just not interested.

💔 **He doesn't want to move/visit/do long-distance:** He may live a couple of hours away (or in Alaska, Pakistan, or Timbuktu, for that matter), but that absolutely does not matter to a guy in love—he will do whatever it takes to be with the woman he's crazy about. If all this time you've been telling yourself, "Well, he's really connected to his roots," or "He's just scared to take the plunge," you've been lying to yourself, and deep down, you probably know it. Guys want to be with the girls they love, end of story. It's really not complicated at all.

💔 **He's not looking for anything long-term:** Have we learned nothing from *The Bachelorette*? A guy wants to find the love of his life. So if he says he's not looking for anything long term, you can take that as an "I'm just not looking for anything long term with *you*." It won't do you one bit of good to tell yourself, "Maybe if we just try it for a while, he'll see that we're perfect for each other" or "He's been burned in the past and is just being cautious." When a guy really wants you, he will want all of you, forever. No convincing needed.

But what about online dating? How do all of *these* rules fit into that world? It's a whole new ball game, which, seemingly, would require a new set of rules. Surprisingly, it's not that different. While the means of meeting is distinctly original and native to our generation, the basic rules still apply. I could tell you which ones, but I think it's better to let a success story do the talking.

My friend Amanda has an amazing account of how she met her husband through an online dating site. She says, "I had seen him at the gym I train at and even tried to get close to him, to no avail. Then, three months later, I tried an online dating site because it was offering a free three-day trial. Of all the e-mails I received, only Geoff stood out to me. We started messaging and I quickly realized he was 'that guy' from the gym. We spoke at the gym for the first time that night, and from there, started talking on the phone for hours as if we were back in middle school. I e-mailed my close friends and family that first week and said, 'Mark my words, I am going to marry him.' And here we are today, happily married!" How sweet is that? Nora Ephron would be so proud.

In honor of matches everywhere that are made in online heaven, I've put together a few **BE**'s to keep in mind when you're creating your profile:

**BE** honest—A shared interest is one of the main things that attract people to each other—a common passion or goal. Be up-front about your activities, vocation, beliefs, hobbies, and personality. If they're interested in you, they'll be interested in *all* of you.

**BE** available—At first, online dating may seem like a tricky place to let the guy do the pursuing, but, actually, it's kind of the perfect place. By simply joining and creating a profile, you're letting him know that you're available. It takes the guesswork out of it. I feel like that's half the difficulty with regular dating—unless you're at a singles bar with a sign strapped around your neck that reads "Open for Business!" it can be hard to tell who's available and who's not. So by simply being open to meeting different people and keeping an optimistic attitude, you're on the right track.

**BE** yourself—It can be tempting to report only what you *think* others want to see, but the real you is best—big feet, crooked teeth, and all. Have a yappy dog? A failed business? A less-than-perfect BMI number? Don't worry about being perfect, just be you.

**BE** real—The best way to really get to know someone is to see how they act in real life—including around your friends and with your family. If you hit it off with someone, make plans to take your relationship off-line. Even if it's not a match made in heaven, it's experience gained. And you never know when it might be the One.

**BE** safe—I know this goes without saying, but it makes me feel better just knowing that I covered it. Most sites have blocks and restrictions in place to protect your personal information, and you probably know to meet a first date at a public place and not give him your home address. Just be sure that you're doing your part to keep yourself out of harm's way.

No matter what form it takes—online, in-person, or some other yet-to-be-invented way—don't lose faith in the process. Your Mr. Darcy (or feel free to insert your own favorite fictional male hero here) may come along soon, probably when you least expect it. There's no magical math equation for true love. It's bigger than us. It's bigger than all of our planning and scheming and wishing and hoping. If a guy likes you, he will let you know. End of story. Until that happens, you can go on being your classy, witty, and amazing self. When he finally shows up, he won't think twice about asking you out, and all you'll have to do is say yes.

## Chapter Eight

# Dress to Impress

"The beauty of a woman is not in the clothes she wears,
the figure that she carries, or the way she combs her
hair…true beauty is reflected in her soul."

—*Audrey Hepburn*

Growing up in our household, shopping was A Really Big Deal. Every year, we would make an annual pilgrimage to my aunt's house in Denver, Colorado, and, from there, journey to…drumroll…the Mall. There were malls and stores near where I grew up, but none of them were large enough to contain an actual elevator or escalator. So when we went shopping in Denver, we knew we'd hit the Big Time. Malls with escalators! Multilevel food courts! Color-coded parking lots! It was the equivalent of Disney World to a family with all girls. Then the best part would commence: the shopping. And we would shop until we dropped.

It's just a fact that clothes are fun. Fashion is fun. It's not everything in this life, but it's fun. And while I do have a tendency to err on the side of comfy rather than flashy, I actually really like fashion. I won't go so far as to say that I'm *good* at fashion, but I enjoy it.

Fashion, by its very nature, is subjective. It's a creative art form, and in wearing a specific piece of clothing, you take on the creator's unspoken commission to make the piece of art your own. We do this in a variety of different ways (Should I roll my pants? Distress my jeans? Wear this hat backward?), but, ultimately, each person's look is going to be as unique and distinct as the individual wearing it. I *love* to see people's different styles. It's so beautiful to see someone's personality shine through her clothes. John Lasseter makes me smile every time I see him in his Hawaiian shirts. It does my heart good to see little skater kids at PacSun. And even though I don't personally have one, I think it's fascinating to see what tattoos people choose to get. Our individual styles speak volumes about us.

For better or for worse, many of us make entire character verdicts based on the absence or presence of ratty tennis shoes, designer jackets, ill-fitting pants, or leather bags. We tend to esteem, promote, idealize, and gravitate to those who look the best, and point fingers and turn up noses at those with seemingly less-than-stylish wardrobe selections. So it only makes sense that we'd want to look our best. But what is stylish today? What's wearable at work? What's acceptable at my cousin's wedding? Where's that fine line between trendy and too-far?

I never met my maternal grandmother, but I've seen pictures

of her looking flawless in her red lipstick and dark green dress and heels at a family Christmas. I'm floored by her chic style, but my mom maintains, "It's just what she wore, every day. She'd be in the kitchen making biscuits and gravy from scratch in a dress with red lipstick." Not so long ago, it appears the choices were a skirt and stockings or a dress and stockings. Katherine Hepburn was considered radical for wearing pants in the 1930s. When she wore jeans to work, they would be confiscated from her dressing room while she was on set. So she would refuse to wear anything but her skivvies on her bottom half until they were returned. It worked.[20]

Thankfully, today we have countless options, ranging from the working girl in pinstripes to the '70s bohemian reborn (love me some Free People) to some '90s flavor (my closet was once an amalgam of Vans skate paraphernalia and Roxy surf shirts—oddly enough, I didn't skate or surf, but at least it was a step up from the Flock of Seagulls–esque jacket I purchased in '89 with *mirrors* on it).

Anyway, clothes are still serious business, and we shouldn't be afraid to take them seriously. Looking great involves many factors, including mixing and matching, knowing what to toss and what to keep, and discovering the most important key to *every* outfit (no exceptions!). But in any case, it's helpful to distinguish between fashion and style.

Fashion is constantly on the move—always changing, always evolving. There are always going to be new trends, new looks, and new ideas, and that's the fun of fashion—it doesn't stay the same for long. Style consists of our overall presentation and persona—the way our behavior, ideals, priorities, and personalities all shine through in our choices of clothing. It's more about presentation. If you're smart, sophisticated, and chic, your attire will most likely reflect those attributes. If you respect yourself, it can show up in your dress. Essentially, it's not about designers or labels or brands, it's about you: how you carry yourself, how you present yourself. Style is about *you*.

While it may seem frivolous to some, our personal style does more talking than we ever could about ourselves—just think of all the statements, phrases, and titles that clothes have inspired: "Off like a dirty shirt," "If the shoe fits," "Don't get your panties in a twist," and the list goes on. And if we think our attire doesn't have a profound effect on how others view us, we're wrong. Besides our values and standards, we are able to make known our political stance, our emotional state, and even our background and origin, all with our wardrobe. An "I Voted" sticker adorns the shirt of every proud voter immediately upon leaving the voting booth. Herbivore status can be conveyed with a vegan, faux-leather handbag. And daily moods can be expressed through "Grumpy," "Bossy," or "Happy" tees. Lawyers wear suits to communicate their professional status, brides wear white to symbolize purity, and beachgoers wear bikinis to beat the heat and show off their bods. We're all sending some kind of message with our clothes. So what is your personal style, and how do you accurately get your message across?

Figuring out that personal style is easier than you might think. To find yours, simply circle the five adjectives or nouns in the following list that sound the *most* like you.

### What's My Style?

| | | |
|---|---|---|
| ♦ Adventurous | ♥ Hopeless romantic | ✁ Edgy |
| ➥ Preppy | ⬗ Independent | ★ Stylish |
| ✁ Mysterious | ♦ Daring | ♥ Polite |
| ★ Successful | ⬗ Eco-conscious | ♦ Simple |
| ✁ Entertaining | ➥ Organized | ♥ Charming |
| ⬗ Free Spirit | ♦ Athletic | ➥ Classy |
| ★ Passionate | ✁ Night owl | ♥ Old-fashioned |
| ⬗ Nature lover | ➥ Clean | ★ Modern |
| ♦ Determined | ♥ Caring | ✁ Music lover |
| ➥ Put together | ⬗ Nonconformist | ★ Trendy |

Now, out of the five descriptions you circled, add up the number of different diamonds, hearts, lightning bolts, lips, bicycles, and stars beside the traits you chose, and keep reading to match up the quantity you have the most of with the style description!

**Mostly stars** ★ You're a trendsetter! You aren't afraid to be the first one to try out a new look, and you're always implementing up-to-the-minute elements in your wardrobe (loafers? taped glasses? overalls? no problem!). You love to follow the hottest fashionistas on Instagram and post pics of your favorite outfits. Style inspirations include Zendaya Coleman,

Taylor Swift, Sarah Hyland, and Willow Smith, and your ideal spots to shop are Urban Outfitters and bluefly.com.

**Mostly diamonds ♦** You're sporty! You love simple, comfortable fashion that doesn't require a lot of extra work, and your ideal shopping trip would be quick and painless. You're always on the go and need an easy, mobile wardrobe that can keep up with you (comfy T-shirts, great-fitting jeans). Style inspirations include Julianne Hough, Gabby Douglas, Sadie Robertson, and Keke Palmer, and your ideal spots to shop are Hollister and Lululemon.

**Mostly lips ⬬** You're classic! You love smart, timeless pieces and are drawn to sophisticated designs and elegant lines and colors. You always look put-together and love to keep your wardrobe updated and organized with classy colors (white, navy, taupe) and chic silhouettes (wrap dresses, trench coats, fitted button-ups). Style inspirations include Kate Middleton, America Ferrera, Jennifer Lawrence, and Jessica Chastain, and your ideal spots to shop are J.Crew and Bergdorf Goodman.

**Mostly lightning bolts ⚡** You're rock 'n' roll! You love the glam, underground look of music groupies and are drawn to rebellious punk-rock elements (band T-shirts, Chuck Taylors) and bold colors (black, fuchsia, charcoal). You aren't afraid to go against the grain and create your own hybrid rock-meets-couture look. Style inspirations include Rihanna, Ariana Grande, Hailee Steinfeld, and Alexa Ray Joel. Your ideal spots to shop are H&M and Vivienne Westwood.

**Mostly hearts ♥** You're sweet! You love elegant, romantic tops and dresses with subtle feminine touches like lace and ruffles. You look for soft, graceful fabrics and colors (ivory and dusty pink) and simple, pretty pieces (tea-length dresses, blouses with pearl buttons). Your look is understated yet refined. Style inspirations include Emma Stone, Selena Gomez, Dakota Fanning, and Lily James, and your ideal spots to shop are Anthropologie and Nanette Lepore.

**Mostly bicycles &#x6436;** You're bohemian! You love loose, free-flowing tops and skirts and are drawn to natural fabrics (organic cotton, hemp bags) and easy-to-wear garments in earth tones (brown, burnt orange, olive green). You look for inexpensive pieces you can mix and match. Style inspirations include Zooey Deschanel, Vanessa Hudgens, Raini Rodriguez, and Kate Hudson, and your ideal spots to shop are Buffalo Exchange and local vintage/thrift stores.

I think one of the misconceptions about style is that it requires a lot of money. Granted, a trip to almost any retail store these days can make a significant dent in your bank account, but style itself doesn't necessitate the outlay of huge wads of cash. And actually, the less you have, the more special things can be. Because the truth is, my mother worked all year long to save money for our designated "Colorado fund" so that we could get several nice outfits on our yearly trip. I don't remember her ever getting anything for herself, though. She put aside an annual nest egg just so we girls could get something special and new. That's the definition of *sacrifice*, and it makes every shopping trip now even more sweet and special.

Perhaps that's why I got a part-time job at a clothing store in college—I was so thrilled to get not only a paycheck, but a discount on the clothes there as well! (The key was to not blow your whole check on the new shipment of inventory that just came in—my take-home pay took a real shot to the gut during that season of cashmere hoodies.) All that to say, if you don't have a lot of moola, don't worry. The key is determining something you *need* versus something you *want*. So if you're strapped for cash, you've come to the right place. Here is my guide to stretching your dollar, stylewise:

### Need vs. Want

**NEED:** One classic black dress—it doesn't have to be designer, just make sure it fits properly and is modest enough for formal outings like a wedding or a black-tie charity event. The best one I've ever owned came from Kate Spade—it was not only timeless and well-structured, it also covered up all my postpartum rolls and flab. That's not easy to do!

**WANT:** A dress in every style and color. When funds are low, spring for one amazing dress, rather than five so-so ones. You'll get more mileage out of one that you truly love than a bunch that you picked up just because.

**NEED:** A classic pair of heels—preferably black or nude.

The style isn't as important as the color—strappy, T-back, or kitten-style isn't as crucial to the wardrobe as the tone. Sticking with black or nude will allow you to go a myriad of different ways on top.

**WANT:** Cute shoes in every shape and brand. My rule is to have a dependable pair for each season, and, beyond that, everything else is just gravy. Spring for a good pair of boots for winter (Frye boots are fabulous), a nice sandal for springtime, a cheap pair of flip-flops for summer outings (Old Navy, babe), and a reliable pair of tennis shoes for running in the fall. That should get you through until your ship comes in.

**NEED:** A versatile flat iron. Good hair can make up for a multitude of sins in the fashion department. You can straighten it neatly, create bouncy waves, or make fresh curls, depending on the occasion. You can feasibly get years, if not decades, of use out of a good flat iron, so it makes sense to splurge on the front end.

**WANT:** The latest accessories for your neck, ears, wrists, ankles, and other dangle-friendly body parts. Those little baubles can add up quick, so stick with one or two options a season. A gold triangle necklace will obviously go with more than a turquoise bracelet; silver fringe earrings can mix and match more easily than a fuchsia ring. When in doubt, go with the one that screams versatility and longevity. This is starting to sound like a 401(k) retirement plan.

**NEED:** A flattering pair of jeans. I know, I know, I usually spend my days in sweatpants, but every once in a blue moon, an occasion arises that warrants my changing into a real pair of pants. And when that happens, I have a go-to pair. You can dress them up with heels and a blazer for a jaunty, outdoor event or dress them down with a tank, a collar necklace, and flats for a concert with friends. There's a reason why jeans have endured to this day—so indulge in a good pair.

It's a fact that we have to put on *something* every day when we leave the house, so it makes sense to wear something fun, memorable, or stylish. Who knows what untold glories and fateful encounters each day will bring (or disasters and calamities, which might require hospitalization—for which possibilities my mother always reminded us to put on clean underwear), so err on the side of "You never know who you'll run into." Why is it that the one time you make a quick run to the grocery store in your high school track shirt and a paint-splattered bandanna, you inevitably run into your boss or an ex-boyfriend? And when you've actually showered, done your makeup, and look certifiably fabulous, you don't see a darn person. Just sayin'...

Another pitfall is buying or holding on to clothes two sizes too small, in hopes of squeezing into said items eventually. Those things inevitably end up hanging in the closet, unworn, only to be thrown out with next year's charity pile. To avoid sad pants hanging all alone, or, worse yet, squished hips and sandwiched sides, let's just buckle down and buy what fits us now. To avoid getting caught in the wrong size, try everything on, whether shopping or cleaning out your closet. If you're really uncertain about the exact fit, ask a friend to join you and tell her you'd welcome brutal honesty. I take my kids with me because, well, they have no filter. I was trying on outfits for an event one day and my daughter said, "Is that one a dress or a blanket?" Suffice it to say, I put the dress/blanket back and we made a beeline for the next store.

I think we're all well aware by now that there is no such thing as consistent sizing. So if you're regularly a tiny 2 and have to pour yourself into an 8 at another store down the street, don't feel bad. Likewise, if you're a standard 10 and suddenly find yourself looking fabulous when you slip into a 4 with ease, you should splurge and buy two in different colors! The key is buying items that fit us *today*—not things that will potentially fit five months down the road after our vow to cut out carbs.

Never underestimate the power that colors, prints, and fabrics play in flattering your shape. I'm kind of in love with big, loud, obnoxious Hawaiian prints. I don't really have any advice or wisdom to add to that subject, I just really love them. If you're not up for XL hibiscus flowers stretched across your backside, though, try something smaller like a liberty print or houndstooth. Apparently, there's a rule that you're not supposed to wear black, white, or any kind of print on TV because it conflicts with the camera. That's a shame because black-and-white numbers are almost universally flattering.

Luckily, they're still great options in person. Not a fan of monochrome? Pick your most gratifying hue and work it! Popular colors change by season, so when the fickle fates of fashion are smiling on you, stock up on wardrobe staples like basic T-shirts in your favorite colors while you can, and take a pass when your unflattering shades are in.

Even certain fabrics like corduroy and wool can have an effect on your appearance (although not always in a good way). One of my favorite items of clothing is this huge, lumpy brown sweater that undoubtedly adds ten pounds to my physique. Consequently, I try to limit its appearances in public, lest I be confused with a muddy Angora rabbit. On the contrary, extremely skimpy fabrics can have just as much of an adverse effect, showing every unpleasant ripple of flesh and patch of cellulite you've got tucked away. Look for fabrics that complement and highlight your figure rather than drowning it or, worse yet, turning it into a tell-all memoir. Yikes!

The stuff we put on underneath our clothes can be just as daunting. Trips to the lingerie store can end in tears if you're not prepared. Unfortunately, all those "unmentionables" are necessities and, if purchased in the correct size, can make a huge difference in your overall appearance. Try finding a store with an in-house expert on measuring and fitting bras. If you have an unusual size or special requirements, Nordstrom has a good selection in-store and online. If you find a size that works for you, be sure to write down the style and size so you can request or order it again. And a few words to the wise when it comes to the fitting room: When trying on bras, use the hooks at the edge, since bras will stretch over time. Also, try the bra on under a white T-shirt to see if it shows through or creates weird bumps. Last, make sure the stitching around the underwire is secure—nothing's worse than having an unwanted metal rod poking through your shirt.

And then there's the beach. We've all been there. Strutting around in bikinis cinched too tight or tugging at ill-fitting bottoms. The beach is just asking for it—it's hot, dry, and provides a ginormous, gratis, built-in bathtub to cool off in. And of course, we've all skimmed the mortifying Fashion Don'ts and witnessed a multitude of saggy pants, mismatched separates, loose tops, and cheek-baring shorts. Truth be told, we've probably all been a Don't at some point in our lives. It's good to be able to laugh at yourself and objectively recognize your wardrobe weakness; then pray that nothing else bags, sags, bunches, pulls, or requires immediate assistance ever again.

One way to avoid such mishaps is by custom-fitting everything. If this were 1876, we could all just stay home with our sewing kits and turn out oodles of custom-made clothing, but I'm going to guess that most of us don't spend much time with the ol' needle and thread anymore. Luckily, alterations don't usually cost nearly as much as you would imagine, and some stores even offer custom fitting, measurements, and alterations for free. J.Crew offers the service gratis on all full-price items for their credit card holders, the Buckle will hem jeans and make minor repairs if the request is within thirty days of the original purchase date, Ralph Lauren does complimentary alterations on full-price Collection apparel, and Banana Republic makes free tweaks for Luxe house credit card holders. Some department stores, like Nordstrom, also offer the service. Wherever you go, just be sure to ask for an employee who specializes in the alterations area; otherwise, those business-suit trousers could come back looking like toddler-size capri pants.

Modesty and sophistication are still stylish virtues, and although we don't have the current influence of golden girls like Audrey, Grace Kelly, or Princess Diana, there are many amazing style role models today. Kate Middleton is so cute and classy in those trench coats. Shailene Woodley always looks effortlessly chic on the red carpet. And Blake Lively looks good in *anything* (it's really not fair).

But you've got to be comfortable in your own shoes. Literally. My clodhopper size 9's would drown your poor little 6's. You've got to find a style and look that works for you. Because if you don't feel comfortable in it, chances are you'll never wear it. When in doubt, take stock of your closet. Purge your wardrobe of any dead weight. Donate unused or unwanted items to charity and breathe a sigh of relief at the sight of your clean, uncluttered space. If you're on the fence about a certain clothing item, consult this What to Keep, What to Toss chart to learn which pieces to hang on to and which to toss, according to personal style, of course.

| Style | What to Keep | What to Toss |
|:---:|---|---|
| ☆ | Vests, belts, boots | Paper-thin halter tops and dated miniskirts |
| ♦ | Yoga pants, hoodies, baseball hats | Free T-shirts and worn-out running shoes |
| 👄 | Jewelry, scarves, jackets | Ratty heels and stretched-out tees |
| ⚡ | Leather jacket, classic band shirts, Converse shoes | See-through tanks and old jeans that no longer fit quite right |
| ♥ | Pearl necklace, dresses, heels | Faded, colorless tops and lumpy, ill-fitting bras |
| 🚲 | Long skirts, sandals, head scarves | Worn-out bags and purses, and used tees |

One of the other secrets of cute-but-modest dressing is the art of layering. Starting with our bum, we probably all struggle with the whole low-riders-and-underwear-showing thing. The best way to remedy this without throwing away all of our 7 for all Mankind jeans is through the use of camisoles. Victoria's Secret actually has a really great selection of long ones (called the Bra Top Cami) that tuck effortlessly into jeans and keep our undies from being exposed to the world (and as a bonus, also our midriff in front). The slim layer of fabric doesn't add bulk to the outfit and actually seems to create a somewhat slimming effect by keeping everything sucked in.

When it comes to our legs, we are living in a great time in history—there's a lot of layering going on down there,

whether it's boots, jeans, tights, or leggings—and I'm personally delighted about this. Mostly because it takes an incredibly high level of maintenance to prep and expose our gams
to the world (shave, exfoliate, cover razor cuts, lotion up, spray
tan, exfoliate, repeat), and even then, mine still never look that
good. So I'm going to ride this tuck-your-jeans-into-your-boots
trend for as long as humanly possible.

Then, of course, there is the art of layering on top. If ever
in doubt about whether or not a shirt is top-friendly, simply
face a mirror and bend directly over—can you see anything? If
not, you're golden. If it's cleavage-city, you may need to call for
backup. While there's no need to go to the extreme of slipping
an unsightly dickie underneath every top à la Cousin Eddie,
a light camisole will do the trick and works great for keeping
your chest from being exposed. Check out Bloomingdale's
for your first layer; they carry several good options including
Hanky Panky and Hanro. Hanro, in particular, makes a good
long-enough-to-tuck-in cotton camisole with cute embroi-
dered lace at the top, perfect for peeking out from under your
button-up or blazer. And it's light enough to not add bulk to
the rest of an ensemble.

Though they're usually finishing touches, it's the little
clips, straps, tapes, and pins that make all the difference in
the world. Granny panties, purple silkies, double-sided tape,
boulder holders, skivvies, clear straps, strapless see-throughs,
underwires, boy shorts, push-ups, garters, shapers, slips…
whatever you call them, we girls have a lot of things going on

under there. It's a full-time job keeping everything in place, and anyone who says differently is lying. Growing up in our family, the weekly Sunday morning ritual of getting ready for church was nothing short of sheer pandemonium. Three girls attempting to get everything tucked in, glued on, and pinned down at the same time always resulted in a small cyclone of hosiery, spandex, and bobby pins—all followed by a thick fog of hair spray, of course. Whoever says that girls have it easier has clearly never tried to put on a body shaper.

We probably all have horror stories of things falling out, slipping up, or coming unglued, and these disasters can ruin an entire evening. We all know by now that it's never a good idea to go without underwear, especially when crawling out of a lowrider vehicle surrounded by paparazzi; and yet, mishaps do occur. If your outfit warrants an undie-less existence or even a subtle, panty-line-less thong, simply practice some transfer maneuvers before you go out—can you sit down comfortably at dinner? Can you walk up steps without tearing your dress? I'm pretty sure I almost flashed the entire olive bar at Newk's one time, so I apologize to anyone who happened to witness that atrocity.

Second, if you can't walk in it, ditch it. If one heel in a gutter is going to send you keeling into the street, you might need to rethink the corresponding python skirt. Or if one lean forward propels your top half out of your tank and into the eyes of an innocent onlooker, you may need to change into something less constricting. I actually knew a girl whose boyfriend went shopping with her when she would try on shirts, and he would make her bend over to make sure no one would be able to see her chest. I still haven't decided if that's thoughtful or creepy. Anyway, bras also have a tendency to peek out from gaps between those two buttons right around our bustline, creating a surprise peep show for the guy across the boardroom conference table. However, that problem is easily remedied with a good ol'-fashioned safety pin, a quick stitch or two with matching thread, or double-sided tape designed for clothes.

Last, nothing is more frustrating and anxiety-inducing than realizing that a button is missing. A strap broke. A seam came unraveled. We dart to the bathroom and are forced to rig up every kind of makeshift loop, holder, and pin possible from nothing but the contents of our clutch and the janitor's supply closet. My sister is an amazing seamstress and can fix up anything on the fly, but if we're not so lucky to have a Portable Abby, it's always a good idea to have a safety pin on hand. Nowadays they have little emergency repair kits available at almost any shop or boutique, complete with said safety pin and a few sewing essentials, that are small enough to fit in a clutch. They're tiny, handy, and extremely cute.

Above all else, there is *one* fashion accessory that should complement every outfit, every day, with no exceptions: a smile. So what if you didn't drop three grand on that designer coat? We don't have to have the latest name-brand duds to come across as warm and appealing. Feeling self-conscious about your ensemble? Simply grin and bear it. A smile can convey so much about your person and attitude. Case in point: Ellie Kemper is always bubbling over with energy and genuinely appears to be loving life. Mindy Kaling always looks flawless with her radiant smile and razor-sharp wit. A smile is the cherry on top of any great ensemble, and we shouldn't leave the house without one. It can cover a multitude of sins, including bad hair, bad shoes, and bad clothes, so if you should happen to get caught looking Not Your Best, just flash your pearly whites.

Clothing is much more than just the threads we throw on our backs every day—it directly expresses our values, persona, and self-image. When you feel good about yourself, it shines through in your wardrobe. No matter what your personal style is, confidence and beauty will glow through what you wear. We are smart, sassy, and radiant girls who know what we want and refuse to let a run in our hose keep us down. The next big thing in fashion: class!

## Chapter Nine

# Less Is More

"I look my best after an entire hair and makeup team
has spent hours perfecting me. When do I feel my best?
When I haven't looked in a mirror for days, and I'm
doing things that make me happy." —*Anne Hathaway*[21]

**M**akeup is a very personal thing. Your eyes, lips, and cheeks are intimate areas—usually reserved for kisses and prescription eyewear. So it would make sense to feel very passionate about the stuff you're putting on those precious spots. I don't know of any other art form that comes quite so close to the *self*—visual art is usually viewed from a distance, and even fashion comes into contact with our epidermis, but makeup is directly applied to our skin. It doesn't get much more personal than that!

Makeup sometimes gets a bad rap for being distasteful or overdone, but it's usually a case of user error, not the makeup itself that's to blame. I myself didn't know a darn thing about the stuff until my sophomore year in college when my roommate took pity on me and my sad, eyeliner-less existence, and took it upon herself to teach me how to do my makeup. I could practically hear *Aladdin*'s "A Whole New World" playing in the background as she opened her kit and patiently explained the difference between concealer, moisturizer, and liquid foundation. She contoured my eyebrows, highlighted my cheekbones, and put little dabs of sparkly shadow in the corners of my eyes. She got out her best lip liner, lipstick, and lip gloss and sweetly showed me how to fill in my lips. When she finished, I was still utterly rapt and riveted. How had I lived my entire life until now with no knowledge of this? This whole world had existed and I had been completely blind and clueless (and still kind of am). Ever since then, I've been fascinated by the power of makeup.

Makeup itself is nothing new; it dates back to some of the earliest kings and queens—think Cleopatra and King Tut. I'm sure we've all heard of some of the primitive ways they created said products, including smashing berries and grinding herbs. It makes our harried efforts to grab a new mascara from the beauty aisle at Walgreens look downright laughable. And if you think a day at the spa is cathartic and rejuvenating, try guessing the lengths they went to when preparing for a big event. Esther underwent *twelve* months of intense beauty treatment before she was allowed to see King Ahasuerus. Talk about pressure! Apparently it worked, though, because he pretty much married her on the spot and put her in charge of the whole shebang.

Case in point: Makeup is powerful. It can educe confidence

and cause heads to turn. It can take you from day to night and help you land that cover shoot. It's not only a creative art form, it's a tool for expression and communication. All that in a tiny little tube. It's also been the source of endless discussions and controversies. Where the rub comes in is with people who feel that makeup is absolutely necessary to your existence. Others are offended that we feel the need to wear makeup at all. And still others get miffed at the suggestion of not taking care to put a little something on your face each day (seriously, how can one little pot of eye cream elicit such a strong reaction from people?). I don't really have an opinion one way or another—I don't wear a stitch of it at home, and beyond that, varying layers depending on the occasion. A run to Kroger? Baseball hat and ChapStick. Whole Foods? Baseball hat and lip gloss. (I reason that the friends I'd see there would care more about my level of maintenance than the friends I run into at Kroger. It's deranged.) But beyond all the speculations and general hullabaloo, makeup is just fun.

The original intention of makeup was to enhance, not cover up, one's natural beauty. There are a lot of great cosmetic companies that still promote this theory. But we have somehow been deceived into thinking that it's absolutely necessary to have everything plumped up, thinned out, and overdone. So we run out and get the biggest brushes, the fattest mascara, and the world's largest container of blush in hopes of compensating for something that wasn't even missing in the first place. The whole thing is confusing, really. Think about it: We tsk-tsk those who have Botoxed their way to happiness, then gape aghast at women caught running to yoga class in nothing but aviators and a hair tie. We gaze lustily at someone with a perfect plastic surgery nose, then begrudge the lady in front of us at Sephora for buying $495 worth of products. At the end of the day, it's just makeup; therefore, I say, let's all celebrate each other's beauty in whatever form that comes in. The world could use a little more joy and a little less hate anyway.

Personally, I am always delighted to see Emily Blunt foundationless and Kerry Washington sans eye shadow. They are flawless even *without* makeup and look absolutely perfect in their natural state. They are living proof that it's possible to look pristine without packing on the products. Then again, it's really fun to get dressed up and do a not-the-norm routine sometimes, too. And musicians are the perfect muse when it comes to quirky makeup styles: Gwen Stefani still looks as fierce and fresh as ever some two decades after her first No Doubt single was released. Katy Perry provides plenty of fun, outside-the-box inspiration when it comes to makeup. On the more natural side of things, if you're going for a beachy, West Coast–chic vibe, look no further than Colbie Caillat. If you're wanting a classic, East Coast style, Sara Bareilles is absolute perfection. Whatever look you choose, wear it with confidence and have fun.

Beyond just being plain clueless about makeup, I also found it slightly intimidating. When I was about six years old,

I remember seeing my mom's huge palette of eye shadow and thinking, *What do you do with all those colors?* It was baffling. I smeared some on out of sheer curiosity, hoping it would transport me into some sort of mystical Rainbow Brite dream suit. The end result was more Groucho-Marx-with-frostbite than Rainbow-Brite-dream-suit, so I shut the lid and didn't touch the stuff for at least a decade. Yet, despite the intimidation factor, makeup and colors can be fun. Crazy eyeshadow and out-of-character lip hues can be a thrill. Weddings, photo shoots, and other momentous occasions can even call for getting your makeup professionally done (sitting at the Clinique counter is kind of my love language). While everyday life may not produce events worthy of that caliber of aesthetic application, it's fun to indulge and feel special every once in a while.

Since that fateful day when I dug through my mom's eyeshadow palette, I've also learned the meaning of *use contents sparingly*. Turns out there is a difference between big-screen-ready and dimly-lit-office-ready. We all know that foundation is more or less a small vat of miracles and that nothing feels more bold than slathering on a big coat of red lipstick, but like anything else, there can be too much of a good thing. If you don't believe me, just google "the 1980s."

Big and bold has its place, but the real tragedy would be in covering up all the quirks and complexities that make you *you*.

Do you have a mole or a beauty mark? Let it stand out as your distinguishing feature. How about full, pouty lips? Don't play them down. One day, a friend said to me, "I can't see your

freckles anymore. It's sad to see them covered up." I was horrified to discover I'd been concealer-ing over them, as that's the
one feature I've got linking me to supermodel Amber Valetta.
I tell myself, *She's got freckles, you've got freckles, you're practically the same person.* All that to say, don't be afraid to let your
unique and distinctive features shine through.

Another great way we can look our best is by remember-
ing an old cliché: "The difference is like night and day." We've
all seen cases of too-much, too-early-in-the-day in the makeup
department; whether it's the new office assistant who looks
fully prepped for an oil painting sitting, or our eighth-grade
selves en route to an appointment with our cute orthodontist,
we've all been there, done that, and got the free Lancôme tote
bag to prove it.

To save face (all right, pun intended), skip the heavy liner
during the daytime and simply dab on some toned-down eyeshadow and a few coats of mascara. You can also apply just
tinted lip gloss for the office and save the liner and lipstick
for dinner out on the town later. Also, rather than going for
full-on blush during the day, simply sweep a little bronzer
around your face and neck to avoid looking like death warmed
over. Lighter tones and minimized amounts will help you
maintain that airy, luminescent, Glinda-the-Good-Witch glow
until you leave the office, while dark colors and thick products
can leave you melting into one big pool of black liner by 4 p.m.
like the Wicked Witch of the West.

A bonus to using night makeup at the appropriate time is

the thrill of being able to play with fun colors that we wouldn't typically wear. Half the pleasure of getting ready for a special occasion is adding some va-voom to our usual makeup routine—darker eye shadow, liquid liner, big lashes. But if we're continually sporting our night makeup all day long, then there's no place to go from there to amp things up a bit. I had a friend who wore her full face day in and day out, and she often bemoaned how sad it was getting ready for weddings and parties: "Everyone else looks so great when we go out, but I look exactly like I do every single day! I can't do anything more with my makeup!" I think the key is making sure there's some room between your big-event veneer and your everyday look.

If that isn't enough reason to make you turn in your wands and liners before noon, the prospect of a guy might do the trick. Besides scaring the poor barista at Starbucks during your morning coffee run, gobs of out-of-place makeup can be intimidating to boys. I've had several guy friends tell me that girls with tons of makeup simply gross them out. Yes, despite our best attempts to lure the opposite sex with smoky eyes and dramatic lips, it might all be just a bit too much sometimes. I think tasteful and tactful is the key. To illustrate...

While I was home sick one day I took in some sort of a reality/matchmaking show. The host set up a too-much, too-tight, too-tan girl with a sweet, down-to-earth guy in hopes of breaking the girl's bad track record of scaring off guys. The host described the girl's look as harsh and fake, rather than bold and sexy, and advised her to tone down her excessive makeup and lay off the tanning bed for a few days. Of course, our young dater didn't heed the host's sage advice and instead showed up to dinner with her pink flamingo press-on nails a-flashing and her denim mini riding up to high heaven. She was forced to keep her eyes only half-open at all times in a creepy, bulging kind of way because of her too-thick false lashes and eye goop, and she teetered nervously on the brink of disaster all evening in her five-inch stilettos. At the end of the evening, the sweet boy dropped her off early and kindly informed the camera that she was a nice girl, but she looked absolutely ridiculous and simply *wore too much makeup*.

The sad thing is that the girl couldn't see how beautiful she really was. Underneath all the gloss and glitter, she was truly lovely and didn't need pounds of products to prove it. It's the same with us—many times we feel compelled to compensate for some insecurity or sensitivity—when, in reality, we are perfect just the way we are. No amount of makeup will make up for something missing (Did you see what I did there? Makeup? Make up? That's about as clever as I get, so I didn't want you to miss it).

Plastic surgery is another topic fraught with controversy and debate. Supposedly, with just a nip and a tuck, things can be flattened, heightened, lifted, or smoothed. I went through a lot of medical treatments and hospital visits while I was sick, so I personally don't care to revisit that world for any reason—aesthetic or otherwise. But I know lots of people are dead set on fixing their supposedly imperfect features. Just make sure you know the risks before you undergo such a procedure. If you're of the au naturel mind-set, rather than reconstructing every slightly imperfect feature, look for ways to highlight your good features.

What is your favorite feature? Is it your Bette Davis eyes? The perfect-pout lips? How about those Celine Dion cheekbones? Whatever feature you feel good about, there is a way to bring it out even more. Once you've established your favorite area to underscore, you can successfully play up that area with a few easy tricks and techniques—without spending ten grand to fix the things you aren't so crazy about.

### The Eyes Have It

If you love your peepers and can't wait to play them up, read on for secret tips and tools for making them pop.

For blue or green eyes, pick up a brown eyeliner and a brown eyeshadow combination package (available at almost every drugstore). If you want to snag the stuff separately, try Revlon's shadow sticks—they glide on smoothly and are very affordable. Or if you don't mind spending a little more, try Lorac's Pro Palette—not only is the shadow amazing, but it comes with a Mini Behind the Scenes Eye Primer. After prepping your skin with a good moisturizer (with SPF!), sweep on the lighter bronze color from your lash line to your eyelid crease, then blend the darker brown into the crease and just a bit above. For a nighttime look, add the eyeliner as close as possible to the lash line and blend the dark brown a bit deeper into the crease. Lightly brush a neutral shade from the base of the lashes to the brow bone. Finish with a couple of coats of good mascara—I try to branch out, but I always come back to Lancôme Définicils.

If you're a brown-eyed girl, look for a deep gray or blue eyeliner and eyeshadow combination. My friend Megyn has beautiful brown eyes, and she uses Almay's Intense I-Color eyeliner. They also have a great brown-eye-enhancing color palette that works well with those liners. But if you're okay with shelling out a few more bucks, pick up an Automagically eye lining pencil from Origins; it really does work and feels like magic, and it's made with more skin-friendly substances. For daytime looks, brush on one of the lighter shades of gray and blue from your lash line to the crease. Then fill in the crease and a little above with the deepest color in the kit. To switch over to night, fill your lash line with the eyeliner and blend the dark blue and gray deeper into the crease. Sweep a shimmery, lighter shade from the base of the lashes to the brow bone. Finish off with a good mascara—if you want to splurge, try Guerlain's Cils d'Enfer Maxi Lash mascara.

If that's still not enough and you want to take your eyes even further, here are a few more not-so-secret-anymore top secrets.

- Origins has a great little product called Underwear for Lashes, and it's practically divine. A couple of coats will plump your lashes and keep them primed for mascara.
- If you're looking for a more dramatic eye effect, dip your eyeshadow wand into water, shake off the excess, and apply the shadow as usual—the $H_2O$ boost will deepen the shadow and create an even more smoldering effect.
- For a perfect brow, pick up the Anastasia Beverly Hills 5 Element Brow Kit—it comes with tweezers and brow gel, among other things!

### Pucker Up

If you are crazy about your kisser and want to make those lips as alluring as possible, read on.

For a lighter complexion à la Alexis Bledel or Elle Fanning, keep lips soft and neutral so as not to overwhelm the rest of the face. Start with a lip pencil from NYX or splurge on MAC's Technakohl Liner—they have a myriad of amazing shades to perfectly match your complexion. Carefully line the lips (nothing inside or outside the normal line—weird!) and then cover all over the lips with a complementary shade of lipstick—try something fiscally friendly from Rimmel's Kate Moss line (which is actually really amazing) or spring for NARS's amazing Belle de Jour Lipstick (so many great colors for us fair-skinned, freckly girls). Blend a dab of concealer in the center of the bottom lip and right under the center of your top lip for a little highlight, and then blot a light dusting of powder like Laura Mercier's Invisible Loose Setting Powder over everything to seal in your hard work. Finish with a lighter-colored gloss from Lancôme's world-famous Juicy Tubes Smoothie lineup, or try one of Bobbi Brown's luxurious High Shimmer lip glosses. Be prepared to get kissed!

For a darker complexion like Zoe Kravitz or Leona Lewis, don't be afraid to go dark and dramatic on the lips. For a luxurious experience, start with a swipe of Korres Colorless Lip Butter Stick (I'm slightly obsessed with Korres). Next, find a liner close to your natural lip color—Clinique has several beautiful shades in their Quickliner for Lips Intense line, or go for broke with Christian Dior's Contour Lipliner Pencil. Next find a great lipstick like MAC Matte Lipstick and cover the entire area. Dab a bit of concealer in the center of the bottom lip and directly below the center of the top lip for a small touch of highlight, then seal everything with a setting powder like Cover FX's Matte Setting Powder. To finish, add a swipe of really good lip gloss like NARS Lip Gloss in Turkish Delight (rumored to be Kim Kardashian's previous signature lip gloss. I don't know about you, but I'd be willing to drop $26 on the off chance that my lips might turn out looking like hers) or Marc Jacobs Enamored Hi-Shine Gloss Lip Lacquer Lipgloss (I'm also obsessed with lip lacquer *and* Marc Jacobs, so this one's a win-win in my book). They're a little pricier, but if you're not spending eight grand on plastic surgery, you might as well treat yourself, right? And nothing feels quite as good as an expensive swipe of great makeup.

If you want to go the extra nine yards on your lips, here are a few trade secrets to stash away in your purse:

- If you need just a quick fix for your lips and don't have time to knock out the whole ten-minute routine, keep a pot of Korres Lip Butter on hand in a few different shades—it's a great moisturizer for your dried-out pucker and also provides a pick-me-up of color.
- If you still feel as if your lipstick lasts only about the duration of one *CSI* episode, try applying a few dollops of liquid foundation to your lips before you slick on anything else, and then complete your normal makeup routine—it provides a solid base for the rest of the products.
- If you are dead set on having the plumpest lips *ever*, look into plumping gloss. I stumbled onto this phenomenon by accident several years ago when I unsuspectingly swiped on a sample at Sephora then thought seriously about calling Poison Control after my lips started to swell up. Turns out there was no need to panic, though; it was apparently just doing its job. Since then, I've come to enjoy Lip Venom Original Lip Plumping Balm—it's the least tingly of the plumpers I've tried and provides a translucent gloss. If you're looking for one with more color, try Jane Iredale Sugar & Butter Lip Exfoliator & Plumper (bonus: It's two-sided and contains a brown sugar tip for sloughing off excess skin).

## Gettin' Cheeky with It

If you have fabulous cheekbones, this is the section for you. Read on for simple ways to make them step up their game.

First of all, cheekbones are one of the more sun-exposed, freckle-prone areas of your body, thanks to the fact that they generally stick out just a bit farther than the rest of your facial features, so be sure to find a good daily moisturizer with at least SPF 15. (Neutrogena makes a regular and oil-free line— slather it on every day and you won't be sorry.) Second, my friend Emily introduced me to this miraculous little primer called Smashbox Iconic Photo Finish Foundation Primer— apparently everyone in the free world knew about it except for me. Simply cover your entire face evenly and it will help keep everything in place for hours longer. Then apply the usual foundation, making sure to blend into the hairline and neck to avoid unwanted streaky lines and to keep from looking like Gollum from *Lord of the Rings*. If you aren't crazy about your usual foundation, try Laneige BB Cushion or Kevyn Aucoin's Sensual Skin Enhancer—the latter acts as a concealer, foundation, and highlighter all rolled into one. Score!

For the next step, identify the top of your cheekbone and then apply the darkest shade of blush just below that. If you're looking for a sun-kissed daytime look, pick up one of the Body Shop's bronzing powders, or for a slightly heftier package, pick up a Tarte palette—once you figure out your perfect shade, you'll want to tote that thing everywhere. To get a great nighttime look, try something a little darker from Laura Geller's Baked Blush-N-Brighten family (warning: it looks like a yummy, swirly dessert, and you will want to eat it). After you've applied the darkest shade right below the top of your cheekbones, blend in a shimmery blush directly on top of your cheekbones, but make sure it's something light and airy. Blend it well and be sure to set those cheeks with a good finishing powder.

To get the cheekiest results, here are a few insider secrets:

🖋 To find the ideal shade of blush, pick a hue that perfectly matches the color that your skin turns when you pinch your cheeks.

🖋 Having trouble finding the right area to apply blush? Form a straight line with a pencil from the bottom of your nose to the point where the top of your ear meets your head. That line will indicate the top starting point for blush. And on the bottom, simply make sure that your blush never goes below the base of your nose.

🖋 To create easy accentuation, pull your hair directly up and away from your face into a high ponytail—Voilà! Hello, cheekbones.

Another great way to look fabulous without overdoing it or cashing in birthday money for a nose job is to know what looks best on you. If you know that earth tones are your thing, then play around in that color group and create dozens of different looks that still *look good* on you. Do jewel tones look great with your skin? By all means, stock up and go crazy in that palette with shades that complement and flatter your lovely complexion. Just knowing what works with your skin tone will help avoid a plethora of cosmetic faux pas.

Am I the only one who's been sincerely confused about this in the past? They say everyone falls into one of the two categories of warm and cool, and they've got all these "helpful hints" to help you discover your specific skin tone. For instance: What color is your hair? *I don't know, I haven't seen my natural hair color since eighth grade.* Do you like gold or silver jewelry? *I like all kinds of jewelry.* What color are your veins? *I don't know, they're inside my arm.* I do know that pastels make me appear even paler and more washed out than I already am, so I decided to steer clear of those; and after lots of playing around with colors and products, I finally landed on a good palette that works with my skin tone. To find out what pigments and hues will best complement *your* skin tone, take the following warm/cool color challenge to find out your best possible makeup shades. Simply keep track of how many A's or B's you get.

### Hot and Cold

1. I receive the most compliments when I wear my:
   a. Red or orange shirt
   b. Blue or violet shirt

2. The skin in the crease behind my ear looks:
   a. Yellow
   b. Pink
3. When I'm out in the sun, my skin turns:
   a. Golden brown
   b. Pink
4. If I hold a white piece of paper up to my face in bathroom vanity lighting after I shower, my skin looks:
   a. Yellow
   b. Blue
5. The celebrity whose skin tone most matches mine is:
   a. Penelope Cruz
   b. Lucy Liu
6. My natural hair color has:
   a. Reddish and gold undertones
   b. Bluish or ashy undertones
7. The wedding dress that would best complement me is:
   a. Ivory
   b. True white

**If you have more A's than B's**, you are probably a warm. Warms tend to have golden or apricot skin undertones and look great in gold jewelry. Your natural hair color may have flecks and highlights of red, gold, or yellow in it. Earth tones such as brown, cream, olive green, orange, mocha, and brick red look best on you. Look for makeup with copper, golden brown, beige, or ivory undertones—it will make your skin glow!

**If you have more B's than A's**, you are probably a cool. Cools tend to have pink or blue skin undertones and look stunning in silver jewelry. Your natural hair color may be pure black, brown, or ash blond. Jewel tones, such as emerald green and purple, look great on you, as do colors such as black and rosy pink. Look for makeup with pink undertones, such as icy pink, navy blue, and frosty shades of lilac, mauve, or charcoal—they will enhance your complexion and make your skin look radiant!

It's fun to glam it up and pack on the shine, but it's equally crucial to let our skin breathe after all that pore-clogging liquid foundation and caked-on concealer. You have to admit, nothing feels as good as clean skin fresh out of the shower, and every once in a while, we should just leave it that way. If we don't have time to hose down at the end of the day, we can always cheat a little (I can't speak for your armpits—just your face) and use a great makeup remover. One of the best products I have found is Aveeno's Positively Radiant Daily Cleansing Pads. (Technically, I guess you could wipe them under your pits if you really want/need to.) I'm personally a fan of the wipes, rather than the point-squirt-and-rinse bottle method that inevitably floods the bathroom and soaks my neck and shirt in drippy soap water, but that's just me. Somehow, it's just never quite as glamorous as when they splash it up on their faces in those commercials. The Aveeno wipes are hypoallergenic and seem to be very friendly to the skin. Also, Tarte makes a Fresh Eyes Maracuja Makeup Remover specifically for eye makeup, and Ole Henriksen has a line of amazing cleansing cloths. If you're particularly partial to the splash-'n'-go system, I recommend Caudalie Micellar Cleansing Water.

I'm all for just leaving my skin alone for a few hours, but I'm also abnormally paranoid about premature aging (blame it on the pasty-white freckled complexion that fries up like a sausage), so I'm always on the hunt for new antiaging serums and lotions. For a cheap, fun slumber-party-esque concoction for normal skin that's easy and effective, though, whip up your own night cream! Below is a quick one to try.

### Cucumber Night Cream
½ *refrigerated cucumber, chopped with skin*
*1 egg white*
½ *cup olive oil*

1. Combine the cucumber, egg white, and olive oil and blend until smooth in a blender.

2. Apply the resulting mixture to the face, avoiding the eyes. Relax for about 20 minutes.

3. Remove with a dry cloth. Refrigerate any unused mixture, but it's best to use it within one week.

The bottom line is, it's certainly fun to glam it up, but at the end of the day, you don't need to. You're beautiful with it and you're beautiful without it. No matter what your tone, complexion, or texture is, embrace it. Beauty isn't confined to one certain look—the beauty is in everyone's unique quirks— the little tics that make you who you are. Rather than covering them up, let them shine through.

*Chapter Ten*

# Have Your Cake and Eat It Too

"Let's face it, a nice creamy chocolate cake does a lot for a lot of people; it does for me." —*Audrey Hepburn*

B elieve it or not, curves used to be desirable. Busty? Bring it on. Hippy? More to love. But somehow we've been deluded into thinking that rail-thin is the only form of beautiful. While the media merrily airbrush away unwanted butts and tummies and models get smaller by the day, we are stuck at home with an identity crisis: Is it really okay to be a size 6? 10? 14? It's time that we face off with our waistlines and be honest about...(cue the dramatic score leading up to a significant line)...our image.

We girls tend to put a lot of pressure on ourselves. That's why I actually don't think the media can claim full culpability for all our insecurities—I'm personally to blame for the majority of my batty obsessions. I sit at home, wishing I had Mandy Moore's hair, Brooklyn Decker's legs, and Gabrielle Union's arms and shoulders, then go eat a box of take-out cupcakes with the realization that I will never be any of them. It's a vicious cycle.

And unless we live some sort of shuttered, hermit crab existence, it's hard to *not* see images of perfectly airbrushed bods somewhere throughout the day. We face the flawless Kardashian sisters on the billboard driving to work on Monday morning and a toned and beautiful sixty-foot Zoe Saldana on the big screen on Friday night. From Disney tween stars to yummy-mummy celebrities giving birth, we esteem the lean and beautiful and shake our heads at those who are tipping the scales. We cheer for contestants competing on weight loss shows while their fit trainers bark orders at them. We sigh in defeat as another actress sheds her whopping six extra baby pounds in record time while we struggle to lose our fifty. It's hard to avoid seeing such phenomena; so, the question is, what to do with our reactions to it?

There's a lot of joy and a lot of freedom in just being you. When you own what you've got—flaws and all—you take the pressure off yourself. Whenever I start to freak out about some panic-inducing hurdle I've conjured up in my head requiring godlike levels of perfection, my husband always calmly reminds me, "It's not about *you*." And by that, he means—it's not about *your* ability to be perfect. It's not up to *you* to have it all together. There's a bigger plan and purpose in life than your capacity to appear flawless. Let yourself off the hook and just be *you*. Then I take a deep breath, wipe my tears, and ask him to go run and get me a bag of chips. It feels good to admit our mistakes and flaws and sins. It's a relief to not have to have it all together. It's actually toxic to keep all those nasty emotions bottled up inside.

My dear friend Barbara is a real-life hero in this department. She's strong, resilient, and a constant encouragement. She's supported her husband through various medical treatments (he suffered third-degree burns on over 50 percent of his body in a plane crash), raised four children (one of whom has cerebral palsy), and has personally overcome a lot of insecurities. The secret, she says, is, "Don't compare yourself to anybody else. Just stay focused on who God has called you to be." And she adds with a smile, "I'm still discovering hidden treasures about myself."

I love that. What if we woke up each day with that aim? To discover a hidden treasure about ourselves? Because, the truth is, you're a wealth of riches. You've got untapped talents, gifts, and abilities just waiting to be discovered. So rather than comparing your reflection to the latest star on the cover of that magazine, take time to invest in the richness of your own heart. Spend time with yourself; find out who you are.

Take a little time to discover some of your unknown attributes—the invaluable traits that make you who you are. Then document your findings. What do you have to offer the world that no one else has? What skills, knacks, and gifts are you hiding? What is something you love about yourself? You're a treasure, so take time to do some digging.

---

### Treasure Hunt

---

If we truly knew how valuable we were, we would never compare ourselves to anyone ever again. It's a fruitless pursuit: trying to fit in when we were made to stand out. My dad has a favorite catchphrase; he constantly says, *"I'll say it again..."* and then proceeds to repeat something we've already heard a bajillion times: *"I'll say it again, that '34 Ford Coupe is still the best car out there..." "I'll say it again, that's a lot of money to spend on a pair of shoes..."* So, at the risk of sounding like a broken record (and like my dad), *I'll say it again...* you've got something to offer the world that no one else does. Your life is worth more than all the gold in the world. Don't listen to the lies. You were made for greatness.

There is often a fine line between just fussing over bodily imperfections and obsessing to a point of sickness. But when thoughts of eating or not eating start consuming our lives, it can get scary. And the hard part is, we're usually the last ones to see it. I dealt with weight issues in high school and I remember my family telling me, "You need to eat something; this isn't healthy." But all I could see was the few extra pounds

I needed to lose. Even though I was consuming only a glass of orange juice for breakfast and a baked potato at dinner, I thought I was still too fat. I wasn't thinking straight, and that's usually what obsessive behavior does—clouds our vision of reality. Because the truth was, I was pretty tiny (Lord knows I haven't seen that weight since then), but I couldn't see past my supposedly imperfect arms and untoned tummy.

Between runway prototypes and red-carpet shots, we can feel an enormous amount of pressure to be thin. But the answer isn't in finally losing that couple of extra pounds, it's in getting *healthy*. Because healthy looks different for each person. We've each got distinct metabolisms, unique DNA, different blood types, and individual shapes to consider. A number on the scale for one person doesn't equal a healthy number for someone else. I respect the tools that we have to communicate physical factors, but I think we have to maintain perspective when interpreting such charts. I remember hearing somewhere that females who are 5'7" should weigh around 125 pounds. According to said chart, I was bordering on overweight at 142, despite having always eaten quite healthy and running one to two miles daily. (I didn't know then that the chart was misleading. In fact, the current body mass index [BMI] chart published by the National Institutes of Health gives a range of 121 to 153 pounds as being healthy for someone who is my height.[22]) But at the time, I took that 125-pound goal to heart and practically killed myself trying to get somewhere near it. Despite maniacal daily workouts on top of starving myself, it just wouldn't work. For some reason, the makeup of my body was not conducive to that weight. It wasn't healthy or even physically attainable. The lesson here is to go easy on yourself when reading graphs and diagrams. You're more than a set of numbers on a chart.

That is, of course, much easier said than done. Between the popularity of fad diets and high-demand gym memberships, body image can quickly become an obsession. Even if we're not being visually confronted with the latest airbrushed celebrity, we're constantly bombarded with weight-loss programs, miracle diet pills, and low-fat menus—which are not inherently bad and have, in fact, helped millions of people, but somehow seem to cause us more anxiety. But rather than racing out to buy the latest workout contraption, wrapping ourselves in seaweed for twenty-four hours, or living off maple syrup and cayenne-pepper water for ten days, let's just start by making small, natural (not to mention rational) changes.

If you don't have two hundred bucks to drop on a detox day at the spa, you can try just drinking the recommended eight glasses of water a day. Instead of ordering the latest workout videos from Amazon, go for a walk each night (which is also a great time to simply unwind, think, and recharge your batteries). Rather than investing in another bottle of fat-melting drugs, grab a piece of fruit for your four o'clock sugar fix. There are many easy ways to get healthy and start celebrating your shape without depriving yourself of every semi-tasty scrap and crumb. The key is in keeping a healthy balance.

My husband says I'm great at depriving myself of anything tasty or gluttonous. But the truth is, I can do it for only so long. After I've denied myself for an extended period of time, I usually hit a breaking point and go a little crazy—raiding the cupboards and take-out menus, pulling out every popcorn bag, pasta dish, and candy bar I've so carefully avoided for months, and then proceeding to order up XL pizzas, buckets of chicken, and cartons of fried rice. Hence, the need for our key word: *balance.*

You may not be as loony as I am, but I think we all have an inner indulger. I once composed a poem based on my undying affinity for a certain member of the dessert family. At the time, I had recently changed my major from music to English and was feeling like a big, fat failure—my dream of being a musician seemed to be over and I didn't know a thing about writing. The English department ended up publishing this pithy little entry in their journal and it gave me hope and encouragement to keep going and give this writing thing a shot. So if you've ever been low, or shamefully downed an entire dish, platter, or serving, this one is for you.

### Brownie

*The guilty feeling that I probably should have had*
*was replaced by the thought that it wasn't that bad.*
*Although not even hungry, to that I'll confess,*
*I ponder what's wrong with having the rest.*
*Soon I have a rationalization*

*that nothing good can come from self-deprivation.*
*So polish it off! Heck, have the whole pan!*
*Soon I'm taken by the nine-by-thirteen quicksand.*
*First two, then three, then they start to fly—*
*the chocolate, the frosting—then four, then five.*
*I'm seven rows in and eight inches deep*
*when I pause for a moment to stop and breathe.*
*Then little by little, I start to slow down,*
*and closing my eyes, I curse the pounds*
*I'll undoubtedly gain from this calorie fest,*
*but I'm this far along, so why not the rest?!*
*Looking around, I see no one in sight,*
*and lifting my fork, I take the last bite.*
*Remorseful, triumphant, and pretty much sick,*
*I reflect on my deed and the empty dish.*
Was it worth it? *I say to no one but me.*
At this rate you will never be a size three.
Who cares?! *I spout back.* It's not meant to be.
I'm a happy size eight who loves a good brownie.

I think the only person who talks about food more than I do is the beloved late Nora Ephron. She loved dessert, too. I like to pretend we're friends: *I should call Nora and tell her about those salt shakers at Candle 79*, or *Oh, you know Nora—she can never have enough butter*... Hence, I truly think she would enjoy this story: My friend Allie had just met a group of new people and one of them asked politely, "So, what do you like to do in your spare time?" She racked her brain trying to come up with an acceptable, admirable answer like "hiking" or "volunteer work," but the only response she could truthfully come up with was "I like to eat." That's probably why we get along so well.

I am convinced that we can happily and healthfully enjoy life to the fullest without cutting out every fry, steak, and cheesecake slice. One of the best ways to implement this old-fashioned sentiment is to develop a happy and healthy relationship with food. Guilty pleasures in moderation are 100 percent possible when you combine them with a steady diet of fruits, veggies, and other healthful foods. Unfortunately, it took my getting sick before I really started to implement this truth; turns out my body reacts about as well to processed cheese and white sugar as our sink did when I accidentally stuck a pair of scissors down the garbage disposal.

Try balancing fresh, yummy things with the occasional slice of dessert. And instead of going on crazed, bizarro exercise kicks, try to take healthy measures in healthy doses, like walking or jogging with a friend several times a week. Pilates is my personal favorite and provides a great strengthening and toning workout while keeping me relaxed and improving my posture. Biking outdoors is also an extremely fun way to get in some physical activity and take in local sights that you might not usually see. And the time it takes to drag out your running shoes and go for a thirty-minute walk/run is completely worth it when you can stop by Baskin-Robbins for a mini cone afterward…since you burned all those calories, of course. Here are a few other quick ideas to stay healthy the old-fashioned way:

- Turn snack breaks at work into walk breaks. Instead of loafing around the break room, get out and enjoy some fresh air, even if you only go around the block.
- Take the stairs. Ten minutes of stair-walking can supposedly shave off up to 100 calories!
- Rather than hitting the movie theater again, suggest bowling or dancing for date night with your honey.
- When stopping by the store, park as far away as possible and walk (just make sure it's in a well-lit area). This will also help to keep your doors from being dinged.
- Walk your dog. If you don't have one, offer to walk your neighbor's—they will be extremely grateful. If it's a particularly cool dog, it might even be a guy magnet.
- Offer to babysit for your coworker. Kids are exhausting, so who knows how many calories you might burn during one little trip to the park? Miranda Kerr credits her sleek physique to a variety of workouts, in addition to biking with her son.

Another good way to keep up a healthy relationship with food is by cooking more. No one loves a drive-thru more than me, but it's not exactly good for my waistline or my wallet. Not only is a trip to the local farmers' market fun and interesting, but it provides the freshest ingredients, as well as inspiration for future meals. Experiment with different cultures, cuisines, flavors, and spices. Invite friends over to help out, put on some music, and live it up. Some friends of mine actually have a weekly "family dinner night"; each week is a different theme (Mexican, Chinese, etc.), and each friend brings over a side dish and pitches in to help the host with the main dish.

If you have a significant other, skip the pricey dinner plates at restaurants and spend a romantic evening in by grocery shopping for the night's menu together, preparing the meal with each other, and, of course, doing the dishes together afterward. You'll most likely end up with leftovers, and they provide a great lunch to take to work the next day. You can also hone your freezer-friendly cooking skills by whipping up a few dishes for friends who have recently had a baby or are feeling under the weather—they will be eternally grateful to have an entire meal prepared for them. Another good way to have fun with food without gaining a bazillion pounds is by baking your favorite goodies on a Sunday night, saving one or two for yourself, then taking the rest to work on Monday to share (disclaimer: This is especially effective if there are a bunch of guys at your place of employment; if it's a female-dominated branch, those poor macaroons might sit there untouched if all the girls are on a diet). People will come out of the woodwork for baked goods, so you might even end up with a few new friends.

Another great way to celebrate food and friends is to throw

an old-fashioned dinner party. Half the fun is just planning the menu, the decor, and the guest list. Google some Sunny Anderson recipes (watching her just makes you smile), or stream a Katie Lee video to get ideas for cooking, decorating, and planning. Overall, it's not as difficult as you might think to create a fun, classy evening for you and a few friends. Here is a quick to-do list to help you get started:

- *Do* inform guests of dinner details. Let them know the expected attire, the menu, what to bring, and so forth ahead of time, via phone, e-vite, or snail mail—depending on the formality of said event.
- *Do* craft a theme. Do red, white, and blue for the Fourth of July, break out your leaves and pumpkins for a fall fest, or go green for a St. Patrick's Day bash.
- *Do* keep the season in mind. Light citronella candles during the summer when it's muggy and buggy. Get blankies and sweatshirts ready for a fall campfire.
- *Do* put guests at ease. Offer everyone a drink, make sure there is enough seating, and see to it that each guest feels welcome and at home. I'm terrible at this—mostly because I'm usually too busy scraping the burned parts off the casserole when the guests arrive.
- *Do* have a postdinner activity planned. Keep a group-friendly game on hand like Taboo or Catch Phrase, or select several movies that could entertain the entire party.

🍽 *Do* send guests off with a little something. Make enough cupcakes for everyone to take one home, stuff cellophane to-go bags with small candies, or keep a basket of chocolates by the door for guests to take as they leave. My husband has usually eaten said goodies by the time the night's through, but it's a nice thought, right?

Besides being inventive, satisfying, and possibly even therapeutic, cooking is a great way to develop a healthy relationship with food. It not only tests your self-control—*will I single-handedly eat the whole batch of dough before it makes it to cookie form?*—but you'll also appreciate the final product more after you've put in your own blood, sweat, and tears. Sometimes, literally. I once ended up in the emergency room after an ill-fated attempt at making chocolate avocado pudding, and, needless to say, I have a lot of respect for anyone who can successfully complete that recipe.

I've heard it said that food is such a foundational part of our lives that often the mere sharing of recipes with strangers turns them into good friends. So if you've made it this far into the book, first of all, thank you. Second, I'd like to think that we are more than just strangers by now. To solidify our newfound friendship and jump-start our new healthy relationship with food and cooking, I've included a few of my favorite recipes for you to try (I would love to hear yours, as well). Some of these are good for you, while others are heavy on the carbs and sugar. But they're all quite tasty and should absolutely be shared with others.

The first is my husband's salsa recipe. Drew's mom imparted all of her kitchen savvy and flavor know-how to him and his sisters, so when he's not doing boy things like growing a beard or lighting the grill, he loves to cook. And, like any sane woman, I let him! This beautiful appetizer/snack may be addictive, but the good thing is that it consists of some healthy, good-for-you ingredients. So feel free to snarf down the whole bowl by yourself if you want.

### Drew's Salsa

3 cups seeded and diced fresh tomatoes
1 cup diced fresh green onions
1 cup finely chopped fresh cilantro
1 tablespoon chopped fresh garlic
1¼ teaspoons salt
1 teaspoon cumin
½ teaspoon chili powder
¼ teaspoon black pepper
1¼ teaspoons lime juice
½ teaspoon lemon juice
Multigrain tortilla chips, for serving

1. Mix together the tomatoes, onions, cilantro, and garlic in a large bowl.

2. Combine the salt, cumin, chili powder, and black pepper in a smaller bowl, then add to the tomato mixture.

3. Stir in the lime and lemon juices. Mix until all ingredients are combined.

4. Cover and refrigerate until ready to eat. Serve with multigrain tortilla chips and enjoy!

*Makes 4–5 servings*


If I had to choose my last meal on earth, it would be a full-blown breakfast. We're talking omelets, pancakes, chocolate milk—the works. Consequently, Drew and I used to frequent the neighborhood Waffle House almost daily and were even on a first-name basis with Kathy, the night-shift waitress. Due to my sick obsession with prenoon foods, I feel compelled to share my favorite breakfast recipe with you: French toast. Seriously, what red-blooded creature can resist the combination of maple syrup and fried bread? Not me. So, without further ado, here is my beloved method for French toast—and I'm not above serving it for dinner.

### Tennessee French Toast

½ pint fresh strawberries, hulled and sliced

2 tablespoons sugar, divided

6 extra-large eggs

1½ cups half-and-half

2 tablespoons honey

2 teaspoons pure vanilla extract

1 teaspoon salt

*1 loaf of brioche*
*Salted butter*
*Vegetable oil*
*Confectioners' sugar*
*Maple syrup (optional)*

1. Combine the fresh strawberries and 1 tablespoon of the sugar in a small bowl and set aside.

2. In a large bowl, whisk together the eggs, half-and-half, honey, the remaining 1 tablespoon of sugar, vanilla, and salt.

3. Slice the brioche loaf into ¾-inch slices and soak 1 or 2 slices in the egg mixture for approximately 5 minutes, turning once.

4. Heat 1 teaspoon of butter and 1 teaspoon of oil in a large sauté pan over medium heat. Remove a slice of bread from the egg mixture and cook for 2 to 3 minutes on each side. Soak additional bread slices in the egg mixture while you're waiting for each batch to cook. Continue to add butter and oil to the pan as needed.

5. Sprinkle the finished slices with confectioners' sugar and top with strawberries. Serve with maple syrup or additional honey.

*Serves 6 to 8*

Let's be honest, this just wouldn't be a good book if it was void of a dessert recipe. And since we've got a female-bonding-girl-power-sisterhood thing going on here, I think it needs to be a chocolate one. One of my absolute favorite desserts to make are these unbelievable German chocolate bars—I'm serious, they will change your life. These gooey morsels of chocolaty good-ness will have every girlfriend cursing her diet and every guy within a four-mile radius eating out of your hand. They are very simple to make and, just for the record, definitely fall under that not-so-healthy category. But once you have one, you won't care!

### *Gooey German Chocolate Bars*

*1 package German chocolate cake mix*
*½ cup (1 stick) butter, softened*
*1 tub pecan coconut frosting*
*¾ bag semisweet chocolate chips*
*½ cup whole milk*
*Vanilla bean ice cream (optional)*

1. Preheat the oven to 350°F and grease a 9 x 13–inch pan.

2. Pour the cake mix into a large mixing bowl. Cut the softened butter into the cake mix using a pastry blender or by crisscrossing two knives.

3. Press exactly half of the mixture into the bottom of the greased 9 x 13–inch pan. Bake for 10 minutes.

4. Remove the pan from the oven and carefully spread the pecan coconut frosting over the baked

layer. Evenly sprinkle the chocolate chips over the layer of frosting.

5. In a separate bowl, combine the milk and the remaining cake mixture. Do not overmix. Drop by teaspoonfuls onto the layer of chocolate chips.

6. Bake for 23 to 28 minutes. Let cool completely (2 hours at the very least; overnight is preferred). Cut into squares and serve as individual bars or with a scoop of vanilla bean ice cream.

*Makes 15 bars*

Since we're on the subject of dessert, don't be afraid to actually order it every once in a while. We tend to feign a polite, stuffed expression while secretly waiting for someone else in the party to speak up for the crème brûlée or fudgy peanut butter bomb, while we are stuck furtively eyeing the after-dinner menu, salivating over the dessert cart, and inevitably fantasizing about that left-behind piece of mousse pie for the rest of the day. So if you're not on a job interview or dining with a dignitary from another culture where dessert is offensive, speak up for that last piece of lava cake. You know that everyone else at the table wants it, too, so be an inspiration and start a chain reaction of postlunch goodness.

Likewise, one of the best ways to keep from overdoing it in those kinds of situations is to have an occasional reward, so that when we get around a family-style banana split we don't eat the entire family's portion ourselves. My friend Erica used to keep a stash of Dove chocolates in her locker at work and allowed herself to have one every day. My aunt buys individual servings of Laughing Cow cheese to help with portion control. I try to keep a few Lara bars on my person at all times—the key is to not eat your stash all at once.

So what is your guilty pleasure? Thai takeout? Schedule a monthly stop at International Cuisine and enjoy those veggie egg rolls and pad Thai noodles. Love popcorn? Keep an air popper handy and make a treat to munch on during movie night. Can't get enough hot dogs? Try—okay, I can't bring myself to say anything nice about them. They are compressed tubes of ground-up hooves and teeth. But my husband loves them, and millions of other people do as well, so if hot dogs are your thing, get yourself some processed nitrate links at the baseball game and go crazy.

Finally, another great way to combine food and fun is by helping others. Audrey Hepburn was a great example of this: As a goodwill ambassador for UNICEF, she spent decades of her life bringing aid and relief to impoverished children in some of the most remote locations of the world. World Vision is another great organization—every year they send out "Christmas catalogs," giving you the opportunity to send someone in a developing country a chicken or a goat for Christmas so that they can have fresh eggs, milk, or cheese every day! Second Harvest Food Bank, a local food bank, even takes donations in various forms—you can donate your time, money, or food as they work to solve hunger issues within local communities.

Helping others with food doesn't need to cost you a dime, though. Just by volunteering to serve meals at a local shelter or offering a hand behind the scenes at a soup kitchen, you can touch countless people's lives. At work, my husband helps wrap Christmas presents for kids in need every year, then delivers them along with a bag of groceries. Other members of our family have volunteered with a local ministry that provides a shower, bed, and hot meal to homeless people. Sharing food with someone can break down language barriers, racial stereotypes, and social walls, as well as keep us from taking our own blessings for granted. Food is a natural gatherer of people—embrace that!

Can you really have your cake and eat it too? Absolutely. We need to stop letting others dictate our diets and start finding a healthy balance that is right for us. Not all of us are cut out to be a single-digit pants size, and we need to realize that an 18 is just as beautiful as a 2. You can healthfully and happily maintain your weight without taking any weird voodoo pills or sprinting a marathon on the treadmill every day. It's not about the overdose of those leafy greens or complete avoidance of that sprinkle cupcake. It's about knowing that you're a treasure. No matter what size your tag reads, you're priceless, and a few numbers on the scale won't change that.

*Conclusion*

# Now What?

"It is better to light one small candle than
to curse the darkness." —*Chinese proverb*

How do you change the world? It's a big question. A seemingly unattainable, impossibly big kind of question. If asked, "*Do* you want to change the world?" I think most of us would immediately say yes. We see so many things going wrong in our world today that we could easily relay a few of the issues that need solving. But when posed the question, "*How* do you change the world?" it gets a little muddier. It takes a lot more effort and inspiration to think of ways to implement concrete solutions on a planet full of very real problems.

At the age of twenty-three, a young woman named Tammy Tibbetts was working at Hearst Magazines and decided to launch a social media campaign after seeing firsthand the challenges that young women faced during a trip to Liberia. The results from the campaign were positive, and soon afterward, she founded a nonprofit organization with the goal of providing an education to girls in low-income countries and creating first-generation graduates. As of June 2016, She's the First has provided more than 1,981 years of education for girls in eleven different countries. The impact Tammy is making on young women's lives is nothing short of phenomenal. "It all started with a YouTube video," says Tammy. "Because of my day job, I saw the potential that social media had to bring people together; I saw the power that was available to change people's lives."

Tammy is a testimony not only to the power of social media, but also to the power of one person's belief. One person's vision. One person's heart to change the world. She saw a need, took a seemingly small step to create awareness, and then followed through with a plan of action to effect real change. Anyone can catch a vision or dream a dream, but it takes heart, courage, and tenacity to walk out that objective and see it through to completion.

And it usually starts with something small. Whenever I would approach my mom with one of my gargantuan plans or grandiose life goals, she would just smile and say knowingly, "Don't be afraid to start small." But nobody likes to hear that. We want the big payoff *now*. We want the end results *now*. We want the fifty pounds lost, the puppy already trained, and the cherries already picked. We want an overnight success story or nothing at all.

Turns out the process isn't very romantic. And sometimes the road to getting where you're going isn't very glamorous. Years of toil, sweat, tears, failure, and disappointment don't exactly sound like the stuff of fairy tales. It sounds like a whole lot of work. So instead, we choose the easy road. The comfortable road. The convenient road.

But what happens when we get booted off the smooth road? When, like it or not, we suddenly find ourselves on ... (gulp) ... the road less traveled? It can be lonely, disheartening, and dismal. Daily life can start to feel bleak when suddenly no one at school will talk to you, when your boyfriend breaks up with you, when you get fired from your job, or when you leave home by yourself for a new opportunity. The road less traveled is called that for a reason: There aren't many other people on it.

I believe that we're at just such a crossroads today. The popular route seems to be the obvious choice—it's bustling, exciting, and lined with crowds of people. Beckoning with promises of cheap thrills and superficial delights, it seems like a no-brainer. But then there's another path—a less-worn road that doesn't look quite as glamorous. It appears to be paved with the tears, prayers, and efforts of everyone who's gone before us. Faint footsteps are visible of dignitaries, presidents, veterans, grandparents—people who've fought for the freedoms we have today and left a legacy of sacrifice, hard work, and self-respect. Ultimately, the choice is yours. Which path will you choose?

Most days I am simply happy and grateful to be alive. I'm breathing free air, driving a car, and eating potato salad from the Whole Foods deli. If nothing else ever happens in life, I'm still incredibly blessed. Then there are other days when I look around and become deeply concerned. I see everything that's happening and am sincerely burdened by the future of our nation, our society, and our children. Some days, I think of the famous conversation from J. R. R. Tolkien's *The Fellowship of the Ring*:

> "I wish it need not have happened in my time," said Frodo.
>
> "So do I," said Gandalf, "and so do all who live to see such times. But that is not for them to decide. All we have to decide is what to do with the time that is given us."[23]

Sometimes I worry and wonder if I was born in the wrong decade. My propensities tend to lean more toward an 1870s stay-at-home mom than a radical, twenty-first-century activist. I find myself asking God, *"Are you sure I'm supposed to be here in this era? I think I could have done much better as a pioneer or some sort of Puritanical monk..."* When it looks like the world has gone crazy and seems like society will never return to a normal state, it's easy to sit around complaining and pointing fingers. The government, the media, the education system, the collective powers that be—are all easy targets; but the truth is, it starts with us. I've thrown my share of stones, but I'm grateful to have had opportunities to make amends and I'm trying to do better to make a positive impact. At the end of the day, it's in our hands. It's not for us to decide when and where we turn up in history; it's simply a matter of what we will do with the time that we're here.

And for some reason, God decided to put us here, right now, at this time in history. A time of tumultuous upheaval and radical revolution that looks kind of scary. A time when it seems that all of our values and principles are circling the drain. But when you consider other instances throughout the past when things, people, and places looked doomed, sometimes the supposed catastrophes actually turned out to be opportunities. The taxations and restrictions placed on early colonists actually provided an opportunity for us to win our independence from Great Britain. Our nation may not have been birthed if not for the difficult times in which the early colonists found themselves.

What if Johannes Gutenberg had decided to give up after being exiled, impoverished, sued, and losing his business?[24] The world of print as we know it may never have existed. What if Joan of Arc had stayed at her family farm and never ventured away from home? Would France have won its independence during the Hundred Years' War?[25] Or what about Winston Churchill? Would he have led England to victory during World War II if he had decided to throw in the towel early on in his career with military and politics?[26] History is full of simple people with big dreams. It's full of people who overcame fears, failures, and doubts to reach their destiny. It ultimately doesn't matter who you are, or where you came from; there is a purpose for your life and an adventure for you to live.

We have a tendency to imagine the worst in dire situations, though. When the going gets tough, our minds occasionally run rampant, conjuring up every possible calamity and horrific outcome. However, as history has proved, crises aren't always cause for panic and distress—they can be catalysts to much-needed change and the stuff of miracles. Some of history's greatest players were born out of moments of great distress. Your darkest hour might be the thing that propels you to your destiny. Your moment of supposed crisis might just be an opportunity for faith.

Going back to the original question, how do you change the world? At first, it seems like an intimidating question. The world is big—more than seven billion people big—what does one little person have to offer? What can one soul do? The answer is easy: You can start small. That out-of-reach goal or impossible dream doesn't seem quite so implausible if you take a first step. That unthinkable thing rolling around in your brain actually seems quite attainable if you put pen to paper and set a little first goal. You'll never know until you try. Our lives are but a speck on the scale of humanity—at the end of the day it doesn't matter if we put out the wrong place settings at the dinner party, or wore a hideous ensemble for that first date. When all is said and done, the fashion faux pas, recipe flops, and failed blogs won't matter; what matters is, did we love well? Did we live for something bigger than ourselves? Did we leave the world a better place?

The truth is, you *can* change the world. One life can change the tide. One person can alter the course of history. But it starts small. It starts with you. It starts with one little candle.

# Acknowledgments

Thank you, Mom, Dad, Drew, Abby & JT, Mark & Patti, Geoff & Jo, Hannah, the Buettners, the Christys, "the Hosseys," the rest of our family and friends, and my PB&J.

Thank you, Caren.

Thank you, Rolf, Christina, Patsy, Sarah, Katie, Sara Beth, Luria, Jody, Hannah, Billy, Gina, and everyone else at Hachette.

Thank you, Amanda, for believing in the power of forgiveness.

Thank you, God, for second chances.

# Notes

1. I Am Second, "Lauren Scruggs," YouTube video, 07:27, posted November 2012, https://m.youtube.com/watch?v=JxZMA6oJuHU.

2. Peggy Post et al., *Emily Post's Etiquette: Manners for a New World*, 18th ed. (New York: Harper Collins, 2011).

3. Rory Feek, "Our Town," *This Life I Live* (blog), March 18, 2016, http://thislifeilive.com/our-town.

4. Margaret Visser, *The Rituals of Dinner: The Origins, Evolution, Eccentricities, and Meaning of Table Manners* (London: Grove Weidenfeld, 1991).

5. Hilary De Vries, "Reese Witherspoon: What You Don't Know About Her," *Marie Claire*, August 1, 2005, http://www.marieclaire.com/celebrity/a140/reese-witherspoon.

6. Amy Van Deusen, "Kelly Clark," *Women's Health*, accessed May 30, 2016, http://www.womenshealthmag.com/fitness/snowboarding.

7. Alison Schwartz, "5 Lessons from Gold Medalist Gabby Douglas," *People*, February 5, 2014, accessed May 30, 2016, http://www.people.com/people/mobile/article/0,20783592,00.html.

8. Lucy Stone, "The Progress of Fifty Years" (Chicago: Congress of Women, May 1893), accessed May 30, 2016, http://womenshistory.about.com/od/stonelucy/a/lucy_stone_prog.htm.

9. George Eliot, *Impressions of Theophrastus Such* (London: Blackwood, 1879; repr., BiblioLife, 2007).

10. "Reading 'Can Help Reduce Stress,'" *Telegraph*, March 30, 2009, accessed August 9, 2016, http://www.telegraph.co.uk/news/health/news/5070874/reading-can-help-reduce-stress.html.

11. Doug Addison, "My Secrets to Hearing the Voice of God," *Doug Addison* (blog), May 8, 2014, http://dougaddison.com/2014/05/my-secrets-to-hearing-the-voice-of-god.

12. Terry Flores, "'Frozen's' Jennifer Lee Melts Glass Ceilings," *Variety*, June 10, 2014, accessed August 10, 2016, http://variety.com/2014/film/awards/frozens-jennifer-lee-melts-ceilings-1201216961.

13. South Carolina Office of the Governor, "About Nikki R. Haley," October 17, 2016, http://governor.sc.gov/About/Pages/GovernorBio.aspx.

14. Louisa May Alcott, "Louisa May Alcott," Louisa May Alcott's Orchard House, 1997, accessed May 30, 2016, http://www.louisamayalcott.org/louisamaytext.html.

15. Jessica Seigel, "Hepburn on a Role," *Chicago Tribune*, January 31, 1992, accessed May 30, 2016, http://articles.chicagotribune.com/1992-01-31/features/9201090858_1_audrey-hepburn-unicef-swan-necked/2.

16. Jane Mulkerrins, "Mary J Blige Interview: On Her New Album and Why She's No Longer a Diva," *Telegraph*, November 16, 2014, accessed May 30, 2016, http://www.telegraph.co.uk/culture/music/rockandpopfeatures/11223174/Mary-J-Blige-interview-on-her-new-album-and-why-shes-no-longer-a-diva.html.

17. "Chewbacca Mom's Infectious Laugh Draws More Than 137M Views," Associated Press, May 23, 2016, http://bigstory.ap.org/article/9c78a263f62140aea4317c03cc4f1672/chewbacca-moms-infectious-laugh-draws-more-135m-views.

18. Amy-Sherman Palladino, "An Affair to Remember," *Gilmore Girls*, directed by Matthew Diamond (WB, October 8, 2003).

19. John Eldredge, *Wild at Heart: Discovering the Secret of a Man's Soul*, (Nashville: Thomas Nelson, 2001).

20. Marcie Bianco and Merryn Johns, "The Most Daring Thing About Katharine Hepburn? Her Pants," *Vanity Fair*, May 12, 2016, accessed October 4, 2016, http://www.vanityfair.com/hollywood/2016/05/katharine-hepburn-style-pants.

21. "Anne Hathaway Quotes," IMDb, accessed May 30, 2016, http://m.imdb.com/name/nm0004266/quotes.

22. National Institutes of Health, "Body Mass Index Table 1," accessed October 4, 2016, http://www.nhlbi.nih.gov/health/educational/ lose_wt/BMI/bmi_tbl.htm.

23. J. R. R. Tolkien, *The Fellowship of the Ring: Being the First Part of the Lord of the Rings* (London: Allen and Unwin, 1954; reissue ed., Mariner Books, September 18, 2012).

24. "Johannes Gutenberg Biography," Biography.com, accessed May 31, 2016, http://www.biography.com/people/johnnes-gutenberg -9323828.

25. "Joan of Arc Biography," Biography.com, accessed May 31, 2016, http://www.biography.com/people/joan-of-arc-9354756.

26. "Winston Churchill Biography," Biography.com, accessed May 31, 2016, http://www.biography.com/people/winston-churchill-9248164.

# About the Author

As author of *How to Be a Hepburn in a Hilton World*, Jordan Christy has been featured everywhere from NBC's *Today Show* to the *London Times*. She has spoken to thousands of women across the nation and continues to write books, travel, and blog. For more information, please visit www.jordanchristy.com.